# SNATCHING DEFEAT FROM THE JAWS OF VICTORY

Best wishes,

Ken Libbey

# SNATCHING DEFEAT FROM THE JAWS OF VICTORY

## HOW THE DEMOCRATS LOST THE 2004 ELECTION

Kenneth R. Libbey

ISBN 0-9662206-1-7



Published in the United States by:

MacLean and Clark, Publishers
1285 Vista Leaf Drive
Decatur, GA, 30033-2735
Telephone 404-636-5728
Email: kenlibbey@mindspring.com


Printed in the United States

Cover design by Steve Libbey/Fuzzy Empire

## Acknowledgements

I would like to thank the readers of my columns who encouraged me to compile this volume. My son Steve did the layout of the book and designed the cover.

This book is dedicated to my wife, Teresa Libbey, who patiently read every column before it was published.

# Contents

# INTRODUCTION

After the 1996 election, I wrote a book called *I Forgot, Honey, Why Are We Democrats?* It had a humorous title and cover illustration, but it was a serious book. In it, I chronicled the decline of voter identification with the Democratic Party from its crest in 1964 and the party's consequent loss of national and state legislative control. The story was not simple, involving as it did the social upheavals of the 1960s, the impact of the Vietnam War, and the emergence of Republican operatives who were clever at manipulating public opinion. Underlying the problem, however, was the Democratic Party's own identity crisis.

American party politics was never more clearly defined than it was in 1964. Republicans nominated a western conservative who challenged the party's acquiescence in the social and economic reforms of Franklin Roosevelt's New Deal. The Democrats, under pressure from Lyndon Johnson, passed the Civil Rights Act and sacrificed their 100-year stranglehold on the South. No longer beholden to segregationists, the party prepared an ambitious agenda of social legislation to bring security to the middle class and hope to the poor. The country went along, delivering the party its largest majorities since 1936.

Then it all began to unravel with Johnson's fateful decision to send combat troops to Vietnam. By 1968, Republicans had found their formula to eat away at the Democrats' natural majority. Richard Nixon and his running

mate, Spiro Agnew, focused on the scenes of unkempt pro-
testers in Chicago's Grant Park, tying them to the counterculture of Haight-Ashbury and the antiwar teach-ins on Ivy
League campuses. In the mind of middle-class America, the
Democratic Party began to look like the party of disorder,
rebellion, and loose behavior.

Republicans learned to sow confusion about the issues
that separated the parties. Moreover, as a generation of
savvy professional journalists began to pass away, the army
of scrubbed faces that replaced them became the handmaidens of this deception. They bought into the Republican
mantra of liberal bias in the media and adopted the rule that
any spin of the issues was worthy of respect, no matter how
divorced it was from reality. Republican strategists saw the
opening and went for it. They would set the agenda for public debate.

In its effort to recover from Vietnam, the Democratic
Party fell into the posture of many football teams clinging to
a lead in the fourth quarter. They began playing not to lose,
rather than playing to win. A formal group emerged to advocate for this approach - the Democratic Leadership Council.
They wanted to avoid taking any positions that the
Republicans could criticize, above all on the issue of taxes.
The DLC wanted the Democratic Party to be perceived as
centrist, and hoped to portray the Republicans as hard-line
conservatives.

Over time, the weakness of this strategy became apparent. To begin with, the capture of the Republican Party by
southern conservatives had not changed the perception of
many voters that it was the party of mainstream respectabili-
ty. Focusing on social conformity issues and using simple,
plain talk, the party's leaders managed to perpetuate this
image. They were helped by the fact that Democratic primary voters were clearly more liberal than the DLC and

cared as much about the social issues as about economic ones. The split in the Democratic Party was more over tactics than principle, but it sent a confusing message to voters.

The Democrats were also plagued by strained relations between presidents and congressional leaders. Years of Democratic control had created fiefdoms around powerful committee chairmen, who balked at taking their cue from outsiders like Jimmy Carter and Bill Clinton. Unfortunately, voters are not likely to care about the nuances of the American system of checks and balances. What they saw was a party that could not deliver on its leaders' promises.

The irony of all this was that while party differences had actually become more pronounced and consistent, much of the public did not perceive it that way. Many Americans, especially younger ones, dismissed the parties as Tweedledee and Tweedledum, and felt little motivation to vote. They expressed their contempt in 1992 by giving 19 percent of the presidential vote to independent Ross Perot, and in 1996 by choosing a professional wrestler as Governor of Minnesota over the Democratic and Republican nominees.

The Republican Party, although hurt temporarily by Perot's candidacy, stood to benefit the most from this obscuring of party differences. Beneath the surface, the conservative Republican leadership represented a small slice of the population, those with wealth and power that they did not wish to share with the government. For electoral purposes, they could count on traditional Republican families of small-town and small-business America, along with their more recent allies in the fundamentalist churches. That left the suburbs, bursting with refugees from Democratic cities. Suburbanites could tip the balance if they lost sight of the economic, educational, and social security benefits they had enjoyed from Democratic leadership. Republicans had the resources to stage effective personal campaigns, and were glad to do so if the reasons for voting Democratic became unclear.

Democrats have generally been at a disadvantage in personal politics, both in financial resources and in the mainstream appeal of candidates. Personal charisma overcame the disadvantage for John Kennedy and Bill Clinton, but such exceptions have been too rare among the thousands of candidates in congressional and state races. Moreover, below the level of senator and governor, voter awareness of personal qualities and positions drops dramatically. A well-known name may be an asset, but most voters fall back on party perceptions in making their choices.

Republicans have understood this much better than Democrats. Newt Gingrich demonstrated it in 1994, when he nationalized the congressional elections under the banner of a "Contract with America." In 2002, George Bush traveled the country with a simple message: the president needs your support and you can show it by voting for Republican candidates. He broke a tradition that presidents cannot help themselves in off-year elections, assisted by Democratic leaders who did not bother to offer a counter message.

The Republican strategy is a top-down approach that perfectly suits a minority party. They focus attention on the national leadership contest where they can appeal to people on an emotional level. They follow up at the state and local level with the message, "If you like our top man, remember to vote for these Republicans who will stand with him through thick and thin. They have no qualms about using their party label.

Democrats could counter this with a bottom-up strategy - tell the story of Democratic achievements and party differences over and over and make it the main reason to vote for Democratic candidates and a Democratic president. It is never done, however. The party label is rarely mentioned in

election appeals at any level. Whether this is a hangover
from Vietnam or the result of Republican intimidation,
Democrats consistently recoil from using their greatest asset,
their history of representing the majority of the American
people against the power of the corporate rich. Perhaps they
assume that voters will make the connection for them.

The election of 2004 should have been wide open for a
Democratic victory at all levels. The peace and prosperity
and budget surplus of the previous Democratic administration had given way to a stagnant economy, staggering
deficits, and a drumbeat of bad news from a foolish war in
Iraq. John Kerry and John Edwards did not neglect the
bread and butter issues of jobs, health insurance, high gasoline prices, and tax breaks for the rich, but they never cast
them in the historical context of party differences. They fell
into the personality battle that Republicans wanted, where
every past action and every unguarded comment become the
fodder of relentless negative advertising. The campaign
descended into a swamp of bitter personal attacks, reinforc-
ing the notion that the Democratic Party did not offer a different vision for America.

Once again, the Republicans had succeeded in framing
the debate, playing the game on their home turf. Rival claims
of who could best fight the war against terrorists drowned
out all other sound bites. The mobilization of young voters
that Democrats had counted on, while substantial, fell short
of expectations. Meantime, the presence on the Ohio ballot
of an amendment banning gay marriage drew a heavy
turnout of evangelical Christians. A state that had suffered
dearly under Bush economics delivered its electoral votes to
him by a narrow margin.

After an exhausting, losing campaign, it is tempting to
crawl into a cave and hibernate. Politics in a democracy does
not end, however. When the dust has cleared, the parties

must begin preparing for the 2006 congressional elections, when the Senate arithmetic will be a little more in the Democrats' favor. Preparing does not just mean raising money. The Democratic leaders in Congress should orchestrate an ongoing dialogue with the American people. Using their most attractive spokespeople, they should explain the party's opposition to Bush's attempts to dismantle the Democratic legacy. They should do it in the context of history and in terms that relate directly to people's lives.

This book is a collection of columns published over the past year on a political website. In addition to recalling the evolution of the campaign, they cover key issues that persist in American party politics. Many of them put the campaign developments into historical perspective. While written from a Democratic point of view, they do not spare Democrats from criticism. If the party is ever going to return to its role as the architect of national progress, it needs to engage in some serious introspection, beginning with an understanding of its history. This, along with my earlier book, is my contribution.

# WHY VIRTUALLY EVERYONE SHOULD VOTE DEMOCRATIC

*December 26, 2003*

George Bush claims that his tax-cutting agenda is a pro-growth policy that will stimulate the economy in the short and long run. One can debate the economic principles behind these claims, but there is no debate about the historical performance of the economy.

Eight of the ten recessions since World War II have occurred during Republican administrations. Since 1948, unemployment has averaged 6 percent under Republican presidents, 5 percent under Democrats. It is even more instructive to examine the unemployment situation that each president bequeathed to his successor. In the final year of Republican presidencies, unemployment averaged 6.4 percent, compared to 4.7 percent in the last year of Democratic presidents.

Lest we think that workers are the only ones who do better under Democrats, consider the performance of the stock market. The Standard and Poors 500 index has gained an average of 14.3 percent annually under Democratic administrations, compared to an average of only 5.6 percent under Republicans. Small business owners who support the Republican Party might be surprised to learn that the rate of business failures and the rate of inflation have been lower under Democrats. Even the wealthy have done better under Democrats, since Republican tax cuts have not compensated for poor investment performance.

When the economy does well, as it has under Democratic leadership, social conditions improve as well. The crime rate falls, as does domestic violence and even teenage pregnancy. It is very important that Democratic candidates focus on messages like this, to counter Republican efforts to distract voters. It is also important that voters see this election not just as a contest between two personalities, but between two parties, one of which has consistently delivered better economic conditions.

# 2004: WILL DEMOCRATS SEIZE OR SQUANDER ANOTHER OPPORTUNITY?

*December 31, 2003*

Democrats are currently sifting through a collection of aspiring presidential candidates in hopes one will rekindle the spark that Bill Clinton did in 1992. However, much more is at stake in 2004 than just the presidency. A decade of Republican hegemony in Congress and state governments has weakened public services and is undermining the gains in social stability made during the Clinton administration. The stagnant economy and Bush's credibility gap have opened the door for a broad Democratic victory, but will it happen? Winning the presidency while leaving Republicans in control of Congress would be almost a Pyrrhic victory. To win more than just the presidency, however, requires a change of attitude toward party labels.

All the stars were in place for the Democrats to regain control of Congress in 2002. The president's party traditionally loses seats in such elections. A stumbling economy had pushed unemployment from 3.8 to 6 percent. A Republican president and Congress had pushed through tax cuts that gave most of their benefits to the wealthiest families. They had already wiped out a hard-won budget surplus, and projections of looming deficits were increasing monthly. The scenario was familiar - Republican government, hard times.

17

All that was needed was a concerted effort to remind the public.

The outcome was familiar as well - the Republicans won. They increased their majority in the House and took back the Senate, which they had lost briefly when James Jeffords abandoned them. Roughly $500 million was spent on behalf of Democratic candidates, most of it wasted. The message never went out - voters were never given a reason to vote Democratic. Even the Democratic base was left unmotivated.

Take the case of Georgia in 2002. Roy Barnes, an incumbent Democrat with a huge warchest, got just 46 percent of the vote in passing the governor's mansion to the Republicans for the first time since Reconstruction. Barnes' defeat might be explained by four years of misguided school reform that had demoralized Georgia's teachers. This does not explain, however, the defeat by a similar margin of Senator Max Cleland, a progressive Democrat and disabled war veteran. Nor does it explain the loss of congressional districts designed by the legislature to give Democrats the majority of the delegation. Most of all, it does not explain the phenomenon of Angela Speir.

When no Republicans were interested in running for a seat on the state Public Service Commission, Speir filed and paid the fee. She had no campaign manager, no website, no platform, not even a sign in her yard until the last week. Twelve days before the election, she reported expenditures of $16.00. Her opponent, a veteran of state politics, spent over $140,000. Yet, Angela Speir became the first woman member of the powerful commission, where she will earn $106,000 a year and make decisions affecting all the citizens of Georgia.

How did this happen? It was actually simple. While Democratic candidates followed their usual Lone Ranger

strategy, George W. Bush and Republican money nationalized the election into a contest between the two parties.
Their message was clear: support the president by voting
Republican. Democrats did nothing to communicate a
national message. Their voters were left bewildered and apa-
thetic, while Republicans marched to the polls and did their
partisan duty.

**The Decline of the Democratic Party**

The stunning losses suffered by Democrats in 1994 and
their fruitless struggle to recover from them are well known.
Less well known is the steady decline of the party's support
since it crested in 1964. In that year, more than 50 percent
of the population called themselves Democrats. Today it is
well under 40 percent, about equal to the Republicans. State
legislatures, once bastions of power for Democrats, have
slipped away, as seen in the table below.

*Democratic Control of State Legislatures*

| | |
|------|------|
| 1977 | 36 |
| 1987 | 28 |
| 1997 | 20 |
| 2003 | 16 |

The political disillusionment of the baby boom generation stemming from the Vietnam War had much to do with
the decline of party identification, but it also reflected a conscious attitude on the part of Democratic politicians. Stung
by clever Republican attacks on their support of the poor
and minorities, Democrats increasingly adopted an individu-
alistic style of campaigning that avoided reference to the
parties. Of the two dozen mailings I received from
Democratic candidates in 2002, only one contained the word
Democratic, and then only in the return address of the

county party. I never saw or heard the party's name mentioned in any television or radio advertisement.

This is a mistake. It is, in fact, the overwhelming mistake that costs Democrats dearly in elections at all levels. Party identification, though weakened, is still the primary determinant of most voting behavior. Presidential elections have a strong personality component, and the name recognition bestowed by incumbency is normally an advantage to senators and governors. However, contrary to the assumption of most candidates, a large majority of voters have no opinion of them as individuals. As voters move below the top of the ticket, they rely primarily on party labels to make their choices. It is thus critical that the Democratic label convey a favorable opinion. If the circumstances are such that a partisan wave sweeps over the country, then incumbency, qualifications, personalities, and even money will matter little. That was the lesson of 1964 and 1994.

It may surprise readers to know that only 10 percent of eligible voters deny any party preference whatsoever, and these nonpartisans are the least likely to vote. Two-thirds of the voting public characterize themselves as Democrats or Republicans, while another 23 percent say they are independents with an inclination toward one of the parties. American voters are actually receptive to appeals based on party differences, but mostly too busy to sift through appeals by individual candidates.

The Democratic Party has a winning message. Eight of the ten recessions since World War II have occurred during Republican administrations. The average unemployment rate has been nearly two points higher under Republican presidents, while average annual job growth has been significantly higher under Democrats. Even the rate of inflation has been higher in Republican administrations. By nearly any measure - business failures, increase in real incomes, even the number of millionaires - the country has been better off under Democratic leadership. Moreover, economic prosperity has been accompanied by lower rates of crime, domestic violence, and teenage pregnancy.

Some of the public is already familiar with this message, it needs only to be reminded. For younger generations, the message must be crystallized and repeated in its simplicity. The national committees should spend money getting it out. Nationalizing the election would be far more effective than tailoring support to individual campaigns. It is imperative that voters go to the polls thinking that this is a contest between Democrats and Republicans, and that Democrats serve them better. That is how the Democratic Party label could once again become an asset, as it must be if the party is to win in 2004. If the label is an asset, smart candidates will run with it instead of avoiding it.

# BUSH DEFEATS DEAN - IS IT ALREADY DECIDED?

*January 04, 2004*

Republicans are ecstatic; Democrats are resigned. Howard Dean is headed for the Democratic nomination and a futile campaign against George W. Bush. Maybe we should start planning our summer vacations and forget about it.

Not so fast. Doesn't the current situation sound familiar to anyone? At this time in 1992, Bill Clinton was little known outside Arkansas. He was not the front runner for the Democratic nomination, even among a nondescript field of contenders. He did not win the Iowa caucuses nor the New Hampshire primary. George Bush was still basking in Gulf War victory, despite a decline from his lofty postwar ratings. The economy was showing signs of recovery from the 1990-91 recession. The stock market had turned upward.

The elder Bush lost the election because he could not wish away an unemployment rate that stayed over 7 percent to the end of 1992. George W. Bush is trying to wish away unemployment now, but it is not likely to happen. He inherited 3.9 percent, and the rate progressed steadily upward to a peak of 6.4 percent in June 2003. While it has declined slightly, it remained higher at the end of 2003 than it was at the beginning. Therein lies the opportunity for Democrats.

The modest stimulus of the 2003 tax rebates has already played out, and the tax breaks that are steadily flowing out to the wealthy will not grow the economy. Americans will continue to feel frustrated at the prospects of finding a decent job or uneasy about keeping one. Even if Gross Domestic Product shows respectable gains in 2004, this is not likely to change the reality or psychology of the labor market. GDP grew by 2.7 percent above inflation in 1992 without bringing down the rate of unemployment.

Bill Clinton understood this, as he did so many things affecting the everyday lives of people. The key issue in the 2004 election is not Iraq. The Bush attitude toward international relations is a disaster, but elections are not won over foreign policy debates. The Democrats would be well advised to let the press carry the ball on Bush's misadventures, limiting their comments to the desirability of restoring good relations with our allies and securing international participation in stabilizing Iraq.

Democrats can win the 2004 elections, but only if they keep the focus clearly on the labor market. They cannot repeat often enough the historical truth that Republican government has meant high unemployment. They cannot repeat often enough that tax cuts for the rich do not put people back to work. They cannot repeat often enough that George Bush inherited peace, prosperity, and a budget surplus, and he has fumbled away all of them.

The voters understand this. They understand it intuitively and from historical memory, but Democrats must remind them simply and directly if they are going to capitalize on the current situation. For all his failures, George W. Bush retains a good deal of popularity. He does it with his "locker room" style of addressing the public. Democrats should not underestimate his ability to relate to the public on a personal level. He will not be defeated by personalized attacks.

Democrats need to give the voters a choice and a message. Choose a party that will serve the majority instead of a privileged few. Choose a party that has delivered prosperity in the past and can do so again. Choose a party that will get the country back on the track it was on before it veered off in 2001.

# AM I MISSING SOMETHING?

*January 10, 2004*

This week President Bush announced his intention to bring America's 8 million or so undocumented workers (illegal aliens to Lou Dobbs of CNN) under the tent of the legal workforce. Press reports immediately characterized it as a political move designed to win enough Hispanic votes to carry Florida and California in the November election. I must defer to experts from these groups to assess whether such a ploy could work, but it is not readily apparent to me why people already established as citizens and voters in this country would cast their votes on behalf of strangers trying to get in.

Immigration has always been a sensitive issue, with immigrants welcomed during economic expansions and resented during hard times. The earliest immigrants from Northern Europe still resent the cultural dilution that waves of newcomers brought after them (not to mention the natives who were already here and the Africans brought against their will). Pat Buchanan articulated this disdain in the 1990s, and attracted enough votes to be an embarrass-ment, if not a threat, to the Republican establishment. If Buchanan is not worn out by now, Bush's latest proposal should be a call to arms.

Controlling immigration is a complicated subject, and not one I care to analyze at the moment. What intrigues me is the politics of it. Immigration is one of those issues that poses a dilemma for both political parties.

Officially, the humanitarian/civil rights mantle worn by Democrats requires compassion for families struggling against the odds to improve their lot in life. Moreover, the Democrats in Jefferson's time were the first to recognize the political opportunity represented by boatloads of potential voters. As small farmers drifted away from it, the Democratic Party became a peculiar alliance of southern planters and northern ethnic neighborhoods. The immigrants themselves, especially the Irish and Italians, saw Democratic politics as a means to enter the middle class, and the great political machines developed.

The dilemma for Democrats arose from human nature. As they assimilated into American culture, many immigrants became intensely patriotic, even possessive, toward their new country. While they retained their own ethnic loyalty, they were not necessarily sympathetic to the arrival of other ethnic groups. In fact, they could be even less sympathetic than the old Mayflower crowd, and this sentiment is certainly a factor today relative to immigrants from Southeast Asia and Central America. A further consideration for Democrats is the importance of organized labor to Democratic campaigns. Unions themselves have difficulty reconciling the threat and the opportunity posed by undocumented workers.

For the Republicans, immigration has always been a tradeoff. The great Republican fortunes were made developing the continent in the Nineteenth Century, largely with immigrant labor. Thanks to the Civil War, which disabled the Democratic Party for decades, the Republicans could tolerate immigrant voting behavior and still maintain control, until the Great Depression swept them away.

The business community, large and small, that controls the Republican Party has always viewed immigrants as a source of cheap, dependable labor. Immigration is a safety valve that keeps unions weak and general labor costs from getting out of line. Many small businesses could probably not survive without it. So the motivation for Bush's proposal is not a mystery. In fact, I would not be surprised if Walmart, among others, were applying heavy direct pressure on the White House.

What surprises me is the timing, before, rather than after the election. By all accounts, George Bush takes his cues from Karl Rove, and Rove is considered as shrewd a Machiavellian strategist as they come. Why then, did Karl let his boss out of the corral on this one? Judging by the letters to the editor and emails to CNN, the public reaction to this initiative is largely negative. Moreover, the hostility is coming from white males who have been inclined to vote Republican for largely emotional reasons. A number of Republican congressmen have also seen the political danger and come out against the Bush proposal. This does not appear to one of those issues where you can say something in January and it will be forgotten by November. If the corporate interests press for this legislation, the issue will be alive in the media for some time.

It is uncharacteristic of the Republicans. Since it was founded by an odd coalition of groups on the eve of the Civil War, the party has shown an uncanny ability to broaden its appeal by distracting voters' attention from its core economic agenda. It has always wrapped itself in the flag, and in recent decades it has used the counterculture, welfare cheaters, softness toward criminals, affirmative action, abortion, school prayer, and gay rights, among other things, to stir up emotions against the Democrats. One need not look any further, in my opinion, for motivation to invade Iraq. The immigration proposal, however, seems likely to stir up the same kind of emotions against Bush, antagonizing the very Nascar crowd that Republicans have been cultivating.

Where does this leave Democrats? It goes against their nature to shirk an issue; in fact, it goes against mine. There is, however, nothing to gain and plenty to lose politically from joining in this debate. It would be better to let Bush fight this out with the press, dissenters in his own party, and organized labor. Democratic candidates should sit down with their smartest wordsmiths and prepare to finesse the questions. And good luck!

# THE O'NEILL BROUHAHA

*January 14, 2004*

Washington is atwitter. The first "kiss and tell" book is out, and the damage control has taken a particularly nasty turn. It seems to be getting more play than Budget Director David Stockman got when he blew the whistle on Reaganomics. Stockman, of course, stuck to the dismal subject of fiscal irresponsibility and did not accuse his boss of daydreaming and plotting a war.

The press is treating O'Neill's passing observations as if they were shocking revelations, so I asked myself if any of them were revelations to me. I have, after all, read some of Molly Ivins' dissertations on the wondrous talents of Bush the Younger. The notion that he does not show much intellectual curiosity is hardly a revelation. Everything I've heard and observed about Bush indicates that he picks up on simple phrases and ideas and makes them his own.

For example, he sat next to Charles Schwab at a fundraiser and apparently heard for the first time that stock dividends were subject to "double taxation." This is actually a dubious assertion, even a trivial one. Just about every form of income is subject to double or even triple taxation when we consider Social Security and sales taxes. But in Bush's mind, it became an evil to be vanquished, and the phrase "double taxation of dividends" became a mantra that he repeated until Congress cried uncle.

Is anyone surprised that policy in the Bush Administration is made by a tight circle of insiders to which an innocent cabinet member like Paul O'Neill would not belong? That Dick Cheney, Don Rumsfeld, Paul Wolfowitz, Condoleeza Rice, and the political ringmaster Karl Rove orchestrate the show for the president is well known to any close observer. Surely the press knows it too, but in today's world of corporate-controlled media, even the "neutral" press needs a "story" on which to hang its revelations of the obvious. What is still not being recognized is that there is no need for debate within the administration because the agenda has already been set by the corporate interests that put Bush in the White House and are gearing up to keep him there.

What about the BIG story, that the Bush Administration started planning right away to get rid of Saddam Hussein? Well, I admit to a little surprise here. Not a big surprise, because one of my friends has been lecturing me about the Neocon grand design for at least two years. While I did not doubt the influence of the pro-Israel crowd that had taken over the Pentagon, I did not think Bush himself was much interested before 9/11. A few months before the attacks, he had thrown in the waste basket a major task force study on the dangers of impending terrorism.

My own view had been that Bush realized after 9/11 that he had been presented with a golden opportunity to assure his reelection by parading as Commander-in-Chief for three years, and all he needed were enemies to dispose of one-by-one. Apparently I was wrong. He seems to have come into office with a torch for Saddam, and instructed his henchman to "find a way to do this." Saddam might actually have been given a brief respite by 9/11, which required that we first give some attention to Afghanistan and Al Queda. So the web of lies that Bush has woven around the invasion of Iraq is even more elaborate than I imagined.

One final comment: the Administration's assertion that they were only continuing the Clinton Administration's policy of "regime change" in Iraq is a lame excuse indeed. The Clinton policy was that sanctions against Iraq would not be lifted while Saddam was still in power. No one has ever suggested that Clinton considered an invasion of Iraq. The sanctions and U.N. inspections had kept Iraq poor, weak, divided, and heavily in debt. Enforcing the no-fly zone was a nuisance, but Iraq was not considered a threat to anyone.

# ARE WE FEELING SECURE IN OUR HOMELAND?

*January 17, 2004*

Howard Dean took a lot of flack for opining that the capture of Saddam Hussein did not make America any more secure. Well, Howard, sometimes it's not good politics to state the obvious. As has often been the case, Dean was on to something but it did not come out very well.

Since the spectacular, carefully planned, and coordinated attacks of September 11, 2001, Americans have paid a mind-numbing price to feel safe and secure in their country. Billions of dollars are now budgeted to support special training and extra duty for police, firefighters, paramedics, and assorted security personnel at the state and local levels (though hardly enough according to cash-strapped local governments). The federal government has assumed the $10 billion annual burden of airport screening and is mulling an effort to monitor cargo operations at U.S. ports. The military budget has shot upwards, along with foreign aid to the two countries we are occupying.

Those are the most visible costs. The damage to our economy, which began with the Bush Administration's physical disabling of the airlines and continued with the perpetuation of a psychology of siege, has been too enormous and pervasive to comprehend. Any enjoyment that may have remained in the opportunity for air travel was washed away in the misery of mindless airport security. To these costs must be added the casualties to our military personnel, well over 2,000 and counting.

One wonders if Osama Bin Laden imagined such an impact in his wildest dreams. Did he recognize the amateurism of the Bush Administration? Did he understand that the American press thrives on paranoia? Did he suspect that American politicians would be too timid to speak up for common sense responses to the attacks? Did he know that all these "leaders" would be his accomplices in thoroughly disrupting American life?

No one in the United States has been a victim of foreign terrorists since September 2001. Only one attempted incident has been reported, the dubious case of bumbling shoe bomber Richard Reed. If authorities had frustrated any other plots, they would surely have claimed credit by now. Does this mean that all our investment and frustration is paying off by discouraging terrorists? Possibly, but it is just as plausible to conclude that Al Queda had only planned one big attack in the U.S. and, having succeeded so thoroughly, turned its attention back to its goal of fighting secularism in the Islamic world.

If Israel, the most security-obsessed country in the world, can not stop determined suicide bombers, how can we expect to prevent an attack on any of the thousands of lucrative targets in the U.S? The right-wing terrorists in Oklahoma City showed how easy it is to destroy a major office building, and they were not even suicidal. The only way to prevent such an attack is to identify the terrorists and apprehend them before they start on their missions. Infiltration, surveillance, paying informants, these are the tools that should be emphasized, in this country and world-wide. The Bush Administration has antagonized potential allies abroad and Arab-Americans at home when it needed both to effectively combat terrorism.

In a larger sense, what does it mean to feel secure? At the end of 2003, 8.4 million Americans were counted as unemployed, up from 6 million when George W. Bush became president. Millions more had stopped looking for work. Millions more lived in fear of falling into the next round of layoffs. Can these people be forgiven if they do not feel more secure after Saddam's capture?

The number of families living in poverty, which had fallen by 21 percent during the Clinton Administration, was back up to 7.2 million in 2002, 9.6 percent of all families. The median income of American households declined in 2001 and 2002, after rising 14 percent during the Clinton years. As for consumer confidence, it was at a high point in November 2000, then began to plummet when Bush's election was declared in December. At the end of 2003, it was 14 percent below the November 2000 reading.

Anecdotal evidence has begun to suggest a rise in crime during the Bush Administration. The Bureau of Justice Statistics conducts an annual survey of households to estimate the incidence of crime. The 2002 data showed property crime leveling off after a decade of decline. Auto theft, a leading indicator, turned upward in 2002. If a rise in such crimes is in fact underway, it would be a direct consequence of the deterioration in the labor market.

Have Americans regained their confidence in the beleaguered airline industry? Somewhat - passenger boardings are up from the depressed levels immediately following the attacks. However, December 2003 boardings were still seven percent below December 2000, after having risen 27 percent during the Clinton years. The airlines went begging to Washington in 2002 and came away with modest handouts. In general, however, the Bush Administration has not been their friend. Its actions have fed the public perception that air travel is dangerous and unpleasant. Maybe it is only a coincidence that no airline has been among the heavy corporate contributors to Bush's campaigns.

Americans do not appear to become agitated any more by the frantic terror-alerts issued periodically by Mr. Ridge. This does not mean, however, that they feel more secure. The policies of the Bush Administration have diminished the economic security of Americans far more than international terrorism has diminished their physical security.

# JOB FLIGHT - WHAT CAN BE DONE?

*January 20, 2004*

We are hearing a lot about it now. Lou Dobbs devotes most of his CNN nightly news program to it. Plant closings and layoffs make fleeting headlines. There is every reason to believe that the loss of American jobs to other countries will be an issue in the 2004 election.

Job flight, the migration of jobs from one place to another, is actually an old issue. The New England textile industry began to disappear in the middle of the last century, as companies relocated to the South for lower, nonunion wages. Eventually, the old South became the booming Sunbelt, attracting all sorts of hitherto northern industries. Some of those same industries have since relocated part or all of their operations to Central America or the Far East.

Transportation improvements have facilitated the migration of manufacturing jobs. Construction of the interstate highway system stimulated the trucking industry and made it less imperative for suppliers to be located close to their customers. Beltways around cities encouraged companies to leave urban neighborhoods for cheaper land and lower taxes in the suburbs. The development of intermodal cargo operations, in which standard containers transfer easily from ships to double-stack trains to trucks, along with the growth of the air cargo business, have made the international transport of goods so efficient that companies find it worthwhile to take advantage of cheap overseas labor.

Communication improvements have facilitated the movement of technical and service jobs. The capabilities of a person sitting at a computer anywhere in the world, perhaps wearing a headset, have increased so remarkably that companies no longer see an advantage to having their administrative, service, and research operations under one roof, or even in the same country. The quality of customer service may suffer, but many executives believe that price is the key to competition anyway, not after-purchase service.

Economic history is replete with examples of one area gaining at the expense of another. What is characteristic of recent times is the speed at which these changes take place, creating the possibility that any one person or community could be a victim more than once. We have also arrived at the point where most job migration is international rather than intranational. It is estimated that India alone has a million people working for American companies.

What can be done about this? There is certainly a temptation to start erecting barriers to international trade. Tariffs and quotas can help to counter the cost advantage derived from foreign labor costs. Buy-American rules can force governments and their contractors to search for domestic suppliers before looking abroad. Tax rules can be written to reward companies for employing people in this country. One should not, however, underestimate the ability of corporations to circumvent the intent of such efforts or turn them to their advantage.

The principal drawback to protectionist policies, however, is that they are a two-way street. What the U.S. does to preserve its jobs, other countries can do as well. America's trade balance has been negative for some time, but a number of American industries, and especially agriculture, have a substantial stake in free trade. Moreover, from a higher perspective, economic insularity has historically contributed to international tension and even war. Free trade, on the other hand, has been a powerful stimulant in a trend toward open societies.

It is doubtful that displaced workers get any consolation from knowing they have sacrificed on behalf of world peace and prosperity. If we are not going to protect them directly, what can we do for them? Certainly, we can make sure that the tax code is not friendly to companies that send jobs abroad. But the best antidote is to follow economic and fiscal policies that create jobs at home. The Clinton Administration pushed the expansion of international trade with the approval of NAFTA and GATT, yet the U.S. economy scored a net gain of 23 million jobs. Unemployment fell to levels not seen in decades and the average time to find a new job got steadily shorter.

Apparently, it is possible to have free trade, illegal immigration, and a healthy job market in the U.S. It is not likely, however, if money is taken out of circulation to rest in the bank accounts of the wealthy. Five-million-dollar diamond rings, six-thousand-dollar shower curtains, toga parties in the Mediterranean, and inflation in the ski lodge market do not create many jobs. Neither does fiscal starvation of state and local governments and school districts, not when nearly one in six jobs in the U.S. is in the public sector.

If George Bush must take heat in the 2004 campaign for job exports and undocumented workers, he has brought it on himself. He and his backers have pursued a narrow tax-cutting agenda without regard for economic reality. The country needs Democratic government to restore progressivity to the tax code and vigor to the labor market.

# IS THE CLARK CAMPAIGN FADING?

*January 25, 2004*

For several months now, I have been supporting the campaign of General Wesley Clark for the Democratic presidential nomination. I have a sign in my yard, a bumper sticker on my car, and a tee-shirt that I wear to tennis outings. I have sent in money, written letters to New Hampshire and South Carolina voters, attended a fundraiser, and even given Gen. Clark a copy of my book.

I admit that I gravitated to Clark by default. I took a look at Howard Dean and did not see an effective candidate. I found him surprisingly inarticulate for someone who had been campaigning so long. I liked John Kerry but I worried about the Massachusetts curse. After the 2000 election, I was also wary of another grave-sounding candidate trying awkwardly to overcome his image of gravity. John Edwards was a mystery. He seemed to have all the right qualities and ideas, but nobody was listening. He remained a face in the crowd, especially in those ridiculous chorus-line debates. The only thing I could say about the rest of the "candidates" was that I hoped they would go away as soon as possible.

Well, OK, how about Wesley Clark? A new face had appeared in this moonscape, and the more I heard, the more I liked. Wounded Vietnam veteran, commander of NATO forces, reasonably telegenic, nice smile, seemed to be articulate and sincere. He was critical of the Bush debacle in Iraq, but where was he on domestic policy? Quite liberal, as it turned out. He was willing to take a strong stand on taxes, which for me is the make or break issue. Not content to repeal the foolish Bush tax cuts, he proposed changes to restore some of the progressivity of the tax structure. He seemed to understand that this was a key to restarting the U.S. economy.

National poll numbers immediately established Clark as a viable alternative to Howard Dean, and grass roots fundraising took off. Encouraged, he decided to contest the New Hampshire primary, which he had originally decided to skip along with Iowa. The strategy seemed to pay off. Polls in New Hampshire showed him moving up from fourth to second and closing on Dean. Then Iowa put in its two cents.

Suddenly, Howard Dean looked more like an also-ran than a front-runner. John Kerry, also a wounded Vietnam veteran, had taken on the aura of a winner, at least temporarily. You could almost hear the sigh of relief in the response of New Hampshire voters to the poll-takers. The real story of Iowa, however, the one of greatest concern to Wesley Clark, was the discovery of John Edwards. The attractive, affable, economic liberal from North Carolina was offering the same alternative as Clark - someone who could compete with Bush in the border states and the Midwest. The February 3 primaries now looked like a major battle-ground between the two.

Approaching the New Hampshire primary, polls showed Edwards moving up gradually and Clark slipping a little. Now, if Iowa taught us anything, it was not to jump to conclusions. In this volatile field of Democratic candidates, voters are waiting a long time to make up their minds. Democrats are so anxious to send George Bush back to Texas that they are weighing this decision carefully. In fact, there may be a long road to travel. It is entirely possible that no winner will emerge before the Democratic Convention, something the press would love dearly.

The question for General Clark is whether he is a temporary victim of a misalignment of the planets, or whether he is not wearing well with voters. I have an uneasy feeling that it may be the latter. I am not talking about the press' obsession with his contradictions on Iraq or his refusal to disavow Michael Moore. What concerns me is Clark's tendency to personalize everything. When I listen to him, I hear a lot of first person sentences. I realize he felt he was unknown and had to get his story out, but American voters are not usually hero-worshippers. What they want to hear is that a candidate understands their problems and is thinking about ways to help them. That was Bill Clinton's secret.

Clark has put forward a lot of ideas that sound good, but he has made the personal contest between himself and George Bush the hallmark of his campaign. His theme is a "higher standard of leadership." Much as Democrats may dislike Bush, a lot of us also recognize the delicacy of criticizing the president - any president. Americans still respect the presidency, and George Bush knows this. He may lose his cool at some point, but we cannot depend on it. Personalizing this campaign carries a considerable risk.

There is still plenty of time for Clark to adopt a winning strategy. Characterizing the Bush policies as favoritism toward the rich at the expense of jobs, health care, and education is better than characterizing Bush as a failure. Juxtaposing Democratic priorities against Republican ones is better than insisting that voters choose between the president and a challenger. Voters will make their own assessments of the individuals in the contest. They will vote against the incumbent if they think it will improve the country. To counter Bush's "locker room" appeal, the Democratic candidate will have to offer something of substance, something that will cause voters to nod their heads in agreement.

# A SOUTHERN STRATEGY?

*February 7, 2004*

This weekend, John Kerry is busy in Michigan while John Edwards and Wesley Clark concentrate on Tennessee. Although taking care not to officially write off the South, Kerry has suggested he can win the presidency without carrying any southern states. His view has been supported by some analysts, who argue that the Democratic nominee should spend no time or resources in a futile quest to make inroads in the South. Edwards, on the other hand, has based his pitch for the nomination on his ability to carry some of the states in the old Confederacy.

As a resident of Georgia, a refugee from northern winters, and someone who has written a lot about Democratic election strategy, I view this debate with a mixture of personal and partisan interest. I want to see George Bush defeated as much as anyone, but I also hate having my vote discounted. I also hate being represented in Washington by a phalanx of conservatives who have hoodwinked working people in the South. So, here is my take on it.

Kerry and Edwards are both right, maybe. For Kerry to win without the South, he must first hold all the states that went for Gore in 2000. Without Ralph Nader in the race, this should not be too difficult in most of them, assuming Kerry runs a good campaign, there are no more national security "crises," and the economy does not take a dramatic turn upward. The nailbiters are Iowa, New Mexico, and

Wisconsin, all of which Gore carried by razor-thin margins. Kerry could theoretically lose one or two of these and still win the election, but it is unlikely. If he cannot hold these, he could probably not convert any Bush states to his side.

Florida and New Hampshire hold the best prospects for Kerry to add to his total. Even using the most conservative assumptions about the inclinations of Nader and Buchanan voters, it is clear that Nader delivered those states to Bush. Taking them back would produce a 53-vote margin in the electoral college. Even taking New Hampshire alone would turn defeat into victory, barely.

George Bush will fight this with a huge war chest, an incumbent's ability to influence events, and the Republican skill of shifting debate to issues where they are comfortable. It is no secret that gay marriage in Massachusetts is high on their agenda, and despite the failure of Iraq to serve its political purpose, one should not be surprised if Bush manufactures another opportunity to play commander-in-chief. Kerry's chances of prevailing will depend on his ability to keep the focus on jobs, tax cuts for the rich, the soaring national debt, health insurance, and education funding. If he can do that, his strategy can work.

What has been said about Kerry's prospects can also be said about those of John Edwards, with a few nuances. To hold the Gore states, Edwards would have to inspire confidence and goodwill outside the South, especially in states like Pennsylvania, Illinois, Minnesota, Washington, and Oregon. If he can do that, as Bill Clinton did in 1992, he then would have a chance to add some states that might not go for Kerry. While North Carolina was not very close in 2000, it might be winnable for Edwards, who carried it in 1998. Two southern states, Tennessee and Arkansas, came within a few percentage points of going to Gore, as did Missouri. Edwards would thus have a legitimate shot at four more states with 41 electoral votes. Kerry could possibly take Missouri, but probably not the others. In short, Edwards' margin for error would be larger than Kerry's.

All this calculus is fascinating, but there is a larger concern for Democrats. Winning the presidency while leaving the Congress in Republican hands would mean that the worst legislation could be vetoed, as during the last six years of Clinton's term, but nothing else would be accomplished. We should not lose sight of this, whether Kerry or Edwards is the nominee. In Georgia, three House seats and a Senate seat were lost in 2002 that should have been won. Already, several Democratic senators in the South are retiring and the Republicans are eyeing the vacancies with glee. Texas Republicans have prevailed with a redistricting plan that is unfavorable to Democrats. Undoubtedly, other House seats will be in play throughout the South.

The typical Democratic approach to such situations is to try to find candidates who can raise money, provide some financial support from the national committees, and let the candidates do their thing. It is a recipe for defeat, as it was in 2002. The fate of these states and districts is critical to the Democratic Party for the coming decade, and the only way to salvage them is to nationalize the campaign as a party contest.

Carrier Corporation recently announced that it was closing an air conditioner plant in Tennessee and moving the production to Texas and Mexico. The plant had opened in 1969 when northern jobs were in full flight to the Sunbelt. Internet provider Earthlink, part of the high tech renaissance in Atlanta, fired 1,500 service representatives and sent the jobs to India. Linens maker Westpoint Stevens announced the closure of four plants in Georgia, Alabama, and Louisiana. The list goes on and on.

Whether the Democratic presidential candidate visits

the South or not, his message and the party's message must be pressed here vigorously. It is the same message: jobs, tax cuts for the rich, etc. It resonates in the South just as it does in California and the Midwest. Instead of scattering resources among a few hundred candidates, the national committees could provide maximum help to all Democrats by broadcasting the message throughout the country. The key to the election is defining the issues on which voters will decide. Will they be Democratic issues or Republican ones?

# ET TU, GREENSPAN?

*February 26, 2004*

One thing I have grudgingly admired about the Republican Party is its discipline. Aside from a few mavericks in Congress, whom the leadership easily marginalizes, Republicans rarely make a public statement that strays from the party line. That party line, which used to come from Newt Gingrich and now comes from Karl Rove at the White House, is carefully scripted to condition public opinion with the Republican version of history and reality.

Democrats, on the other hand, have a long history of embarrassing their leaders with their personal takes on issues. Turf wars were institutionalized during the many years that Democrats controlled the Congress, as committee chairman routinely ignored pleas from Democratic presidents to help deliver on campaign promises. Jimmy Carter's loss in 1980 was due in part to a public perception that he could not work with his own party in Congress. The failure of a Democratic Congress to pass the Clinton health insurance plan made the party look ineffectual and led to a massive defeat by Gingrich and his "Contract with America."

Republicans have generally not had to worry about mixed messages since the demise of liberal Republicanism in the 1970s. Hence, it is remarkable to see a rash of unguarded comments by Bush Administration officials and other high-placed Republicans. The president must be reluctant to get up in the morning, wondering which new Brutus is waiting in the wings. Democrats, on the other hand, seem almost bewildered on how to react to these gifts from unlikely sources.

First, there was Paul O'Neill, Bush's erstwhile Secretary of the Treasury. O'Neill had apparently missed Republican basic training, because he assumed that probing discussions would precede any major policy decisions. He was thus unprepared for meetings intended to make sure that everyone in the administration had marching orders and knew how to explain them. He was also astonished that Saddam Hussein was targeted at the first national security meeting, with only a suitable rationale needed for the invasion.

After he was fired, O'Neill spilled his story to a reporter who was writing a book. He characterized Bush as a "blind man in a room full of deaf people," a curious metaphor that provided a few days fodder to a news-hungry media. The White House machine went into action and quickly portrayed O'Neill as a naïve amateur who was bitter about not being treated as a major player. Nothing is more damning in Washington than being seen as naïve, so the O'Neill story was soon buried.

You would think that everybody would get the message. Alas, along came David Kay, chief of the inspection team scouring Iraq for some clue that Saddam had chemical, biological, or nuclear weapons. Having spent millions of dollars trying to prove that UN inspectors had missed something, Kay concluded that they had not, that the "weapons of mass destruction" were a figment of our imagination. Ever the good soldier, he blamed the fiasco on intelligence failures rather than willful deception. At this, CIA Director George Tenet sprung to the podium to declare that he had never characterized Saddam as an imminent threat to anybody.

Bush, Tenet, Defense Secretary Rumsfeld, and others

tried to plead the case that even the sketchy intelligence they had justified the invasion. The American people, however, were no longer buying it. A large majority told pollsters they thought the war was unnecessary. The Administration was acquiring a credibility gap.

Next came the president's budget director. He had done some calculations and found that the new Medicare drug benefit would cost at least 30 percent more than Congress had been told, and moreover that the FY 2004 deficit was going to soar above $500 billion. This rankled even the Republican backbenchers in House, who had reluctantly voted for a social benefit because they were told Bush needed it in Florida. The press talked about a simmering conservative revolt, but it would probably be little more than grumbling. Bush's credibility, however, had taken another hit.

As that dust was clearing, Bush's chief economic advisor, an earnest and hitherto obscure young man, took the stage. In an annual report that the president surely signed without reading, he projected 2.6 million new jobs in this election year. The report went on to comment that outsourcing American jobs to India and other third world countries was good for our economy because it allowed U.S. companies to be more competitive. Within 24 hours, Administration officials were putting miles between themselves and the economic report. Bush, however, seemed puzzled at the controversy. He pleaded that he was not a "statistician or predictor," but that he thought the economy was doing better. He expressed confidence in his Chief Economist.

Bush then decided to go on the attack by addressing the Republican governors who were gathered in Washington. He gave a clever speech, took a few simple questions, and left things in the hands of some cabinet members. It fell to the Secretary of Education to fend off the governors' complaints about the "No Child Left Behind" mandates. In frustration, he lashed out at the National Education Association, calling it a "terrorist organization." Bush treated the incident like a slip of the tongue and stood by his Secretary. This left the Administration on record as having insulted the nation's teachers, for whom it had shown little respect anyway.

Now comes Alan Greenspan, Chairman of the Federal Reserve Board, who normally speaks in such contorted sentences that he cannot be held responsible for anything. Greenspan has been almost consistently wrong in his management of monetary policy, yet he continues to enjoy unaccountable deference. An unrepentant Republican, he should have been "outed" when he endorsed the first round of Bush tax cuts, making a mockery of fiscal responsibility.

Greenspan probably did not intend to re-ignite the controversy over Social Security benefits. He was probably just groping for a way to save the Bush tax cuts while acknowledging the danger of runaway budget deficits. By opting for future benefit cuts rather than admitting that the tax cuts were foolish, he opened a political Pandora's box. Bush, again caught off guard, said he did not favor cutting benefits for people already retired or close to retirement. That must have sent a collective shudder through the ranks of politically astute Republicans.

Democrats have never been adept at seizing opportunities, but how can they fumble these? They have been given enough ammunition in the past few months for a dozen sound bites. "We now know that the Bush Administration planned the invasion of Iraq long before 9/11, and was just looking for a pretext to sell it to the American people." "Whether it's weapons in Iraq, the size of the budget deficit, or the number of jobs they're going to create, the Bush Administration has a credibility gap big enough to drive a tank through." "The Secretary of Education insulted the nation's teachers and didn't even get a slap on the wrist from the Bush White House." "President Bush sent a report to Congress saying that the outsourcing of jobs to other countries was good for the American economy. I suggest we outsource him back to Texas." "How are we going to pay for these massive tax cuts for the rich? Apparently, the plan is to cut Social Security and Medicare benefits. Is anyone surprised that this is the real Republican agenda?"

And so on.

# OK, THAT'S ENOUGH

*February 29, 2004*

Like a good political junkie, I watched the Democratic debate in California on Thursday night. This morning, I started watching a rebroadcast of the debate in New York, but I soon turned it off. It began to sound like the shouting matches that replaced serious discussion shows several years ago.

John Edwards, desperate to give voters some reason to choose him over John Kerry, had abandoned his "positive alternative to Bush" campaign and was taking jabs at Kerry's record on foreign trade and status as a Washington insider. Kerry was returning the fire by questioning the sincerity of Edwards' recent campaign themes. Dennis Kucinich and Al Sharpton, who have provided nothing but comic relief to the debates, were raving about being ignored. In truth, they have not been ignored but should have been.

Now, I realize that few normal people bother to watch these things. My Sunday paper in Atlanta headlined the contest between Kerry and Edwards as one of style rather than substance, and played up the smiles instead of the barbs. The press has already nominated Edwards for Vice-president on a Kerry ticket. So these two debates will have minimal effect on public opinion, probably imperceptible. They were, however, a clear signal that the Democratic primary campaign had run its useful course.

The primary campaign has accomplished a remarkable feat up to now. It has pushed a sitting president, a "war president" no less, into the background and given voice to a chorus of criticism about his performance. It has given the media, hitherto timid about questioning a Republican president's version of events, a green light to drive into his credibility gap. It has energized Democratic voters, who wondered in 2002 whether they had a team in the field at all to contest the Republican juggernaut. It has aroused the interest of independent and even Republican voters to reconsider what they got for their money in 2000. The result, perhaps temporary, has been to vault the leading Democratic contenders into sizable leads over President Bush.

I will vote for John Kerry in the Georgia primary on Tuesday. I have wandered to this conclusion, beginning with a curiosity about Howard Dean and the stir he was causing. For a time, I supported Gen. Wesley Clark as an alternative to Dean. When Clark dropped out, I contributed to Edwards' campaign, partly because I thought he would have broader appeal than Kerry in November and partly because I wanted the primary battle to continue. But this past week has convinced me that the contest has peaked as an asset to the Democratic Party and there is nowhere to go but down.

The voters in Iowa sent a message that until now has characterized the campaign: stand up to the Republicans but speak no evil of fellow Democrats. Edwards has been the poster boy for that message, but he has reached the point where second-place finishes are just losses. With polls telling him that nice guys finish second, he has come out swinging. He will find that it does not help, and he will only diminish his future in the party. The time has come for grace, not acrimony.

The primary campaign has given Democrats an opportunity to articulate voter dissatisfaction with the Bush

Administration. It has given people around the country an occasion to think and talk about our national situation, about the war and the economy and the arrogant attitude of those in charge of government and corporate America. But that is only half the battle. Now that people are willing to listen, Democrats must offer some answers, and they must do so with a single voice. Quibbling over each other's records will be just a distraction.

Despite the president's efforts to put a good face on the economic situation, most Americans know that something is wrong. It is up to Democrats to give a logical voice to the disquiet. Republicans gained an advantage in the economic debate by repeating ad nauseum that taking money from government and giving it to taxpayers will strengthen the economy. The public seems to understand that it's not that simple, and Democrats should not concede the point.

Nearly one of every six jobs in the U.S. is a government job, federal, state, local, or school district. Millions more jobs depend on government grants and contracts. Unemployment in this sector has the same negative impact on purchasing power as unemployment in any other sector. When taxes are cut simply to satisfy a political agenda, especially when the bulk of the benefits go to a small wealthy minority, much of the money is taken out of circulation. What few jobs are created pale in comparison to the job-creating effect of government spending.

Income from employment goes into a family's budget and increases the pace of economic activity. In effect, "demand-side" economics is not the hoax that "supply-side" economics is. Job creation begets job creation - that was one of the lessons of the Clinton Administration. The way to turn the economy around is to repeal the tax cuts given to the affluent and put that money to work providing the public services that most people want and expect. Yes, wealthy taxpayers will transfer some of their income to the poor and the middle class, but a robust economy will return their investment with interest.

Democrats will improve their chances to elect a president and congressional majority if they confront this issue with the abundant data that is available. Much of the public realizes that the economy has done better under Democratic government, it is up to the party's candidates to explain why. The same approach is needed with regard to other key issues, as will be shown in future columns.

# THE ATTACK BEGINS

*March 5, 2004*

With the president's poll numbers slipping and all eyes on
the Democratic primary race, the Bush people were surely
itching to throw some punches of their own. John Kerry's
virtual sweep of Super Tuesday gave the green light. Roll out
those ads and put the heavyweights on television.

The first advertising was benign, one could even say
meaningless, but Bush and other spokespeople got their
sound bites on the air and signaled the strategy they planned
to use. Their major theme was Kerry's inconsistency and his
votes against defense spending. They also characterized him
as the most liberal member of the Senate, which would be
hard to achieve if he is really inconsistent. These are just the
opening salvos, of course. The death penalty, the gay marriage amendment, and plans to raise taxes are high on the
list, along with a lot of scurrilous stuff that will be spread
on the internet. Most of all, Republicans want to personalize
the campaign.

The accepted Democratic strategy to counter this is to
respond quickly with clarifications and complaints. Kerry's
voting record will surely be distorted, of course. The process
of amending legislation in the Senate, of positing
Democratic proposals against Republican ones, of creating
sham votes for publicity purposes, is so convoluted that one
could make any Senator appear to be for and against everything. Straightening all this out for the public would be the

equivalent of conducting a political science course.

Moreover, the problem with the quick-response strategy is that the campaign dialogue progressively shifts to the Republican choice of issues. The broadcast media lives off the charge-and-response breed of campaigning. Fifteen seconds for the charge, fifteen for the response. Fifteen-second lead, fifteen-second wrap, nice clean one-minute story. If desired, another minute for your correspondent or resident pundit. So Democrats will have fifteen seconds of free air time, a little more if they use a long sentence. Do they want to spend all of their slots talking about issues chosen by the Republicans?

Is there a different way to respond, a way to depersonalize the game and turn it to the Democrats' advantage? There are actually two ways, which can be chosen in appropriate situations. The first is ridicule. If the charge is non-support of defense spending, for example, Kerry could comment. "Considering that our alliances are in a shambles, Iraq is in danger of falling into chaos, and the American dollar has lost a third of its value, I'm surprised the Republicans even want to talk about national security."

The second approach is to quickly change the subject. If asked about gay marriage, a Democrat can respond, "Amending the Constitution is a very serious thing. You don't just throw it out there in order to win an election. The American people know what this election is about - it's about the loss of jobs, the loss of health insurance, and the loss of international goodwill. I don't think people are going to be fooled by Republican tactics."

In every speech Democrats give, they should begin with something like, "The Republican propaganda machine is in full swing. It is trying to get the American people to think about anything except the loss of jobs, tax cuts for the rich, and the disastrous foreign policy of the Bush

Administration. This time, the American people are not buying it." The key is to speak for the American people, not to them. A lot of people are angry, anxious, or concerned. Democrats can articulate those feelings and, in the process, dismiss the slant that Republicans are trying to put on the campaign. Invoking public opinion as your ally enhances the credibility of your position and diminishes that of your opponent.

Democrats have an enormous opportunity staring at them in 2004. Everyone is predicting a close election, but the raw materials are there for a landslide that could deliver the Congress along with the presidency. Of course, events beyond the Democratic candidate's control could interfere, and the Republicans are not above creating an event. Whether Democratic candidates themselves will miss the opportunity depends on whether they can impose their own definition of the issues on the campaign dialogue.

# OFFENSE OR DEFENSE?

*March 20, 2004*

Football and basketball coaches believe that the best offense is a good defense, unless they believe that the best defense is a good offense. We are seeing a lot of offense and defense in the presidential campaign already, and we still have more than seven months to go. Given the amount of money the Bush campaign has and its absence of any accomplishments to talk about, we can expect a steady drumbeat of offense against Senator Kerry.

The Republicans are clever on offense. They know that the charge gets more attention than the rebuttal. Neither actually registers very much until the final weeks of the campaign, so they are not looking for lasting impact at this point. What they want is to throw Kerry off track. They want his fifteen seconds a day consumed by his response to a subject chosen by the Bush campaign. They are hoping he will lose his cool on occasion and show an irascible side to the public. Most of all, they do not want his fifteen seconds to be about jobs, tax cuts for the rich, health care, or education.

Among Democratic political operatives, it is an axiom that the Dukakis campaign failed because it did not respond to Republican attacks and the Clinton campaign succeeded because of its rapid response. They forget that in his reelection campaign, Clinton treated Bob Dole with kid gloves, refusing even to acknowledge his charges. Being a student of history, Clinton knew that the context of the campaign is important and that generals are always fighting the last war.

I am not suggesting that George Bush be treated with kid gloves, or that Republican charges be ignored. It is critical, however, to keep control of the debate. What a truly good coach will tell you is to play to your strengths and your opponent's weaknesses. Bush has multiple weaknesses, but he also has strengths. First of all, he is president and commander-in-chief. His growing credibility gap is eroding this advantage, but it still carries weight. Secondly, Bush retains his down-to-earth persona that probably appeals to people more than Kerry's earnestness.

Allowing the campaign to become a personality contest would be playing to Bush's strength. Consistently mentioning the president puts the focus on the personal contest. Franklin Roosevelt always campaigned against anonymous evil and never mentioned his opponent. Kerry does have to project himself, of course, and he can do this with TV spots that use testimonials from former military buddies and show him informally with his family. But he should use his sound bites to contrast his policies with the failures of the administration.

How can Kerry blunt the Republican attacks and still retain the initiative? First, he should miss no opportunity to use the phrases that increasingly define the Bush Administration in the public mind, since repetition is one of the necessary evils of campaigning. Preferably, he can use them to question what the Republican insiders care about: "Are tax cuts for the rich the only thing these people care about? Do they even care about the loss of American jobs, the rising cost of health care, the crushing budget deficits that are threatening our standard of living?"

Secondly, Kerry can make a virtue of necessity. Instead of explaining why he voted for the Iraq war, he can give speeches in which he characterizes the resolution as an effort by Congress to assure that we would support U.N. weapons inspectors and assemble a broad international coalition before resorting to military action. Instead of explaining why he voted against the $87 billion supplemental appropriation, he can assert that he voted for an amendment to provide $87 billion for our troops and reconstruction in Iraq, to be paid for by repealing the tax cuts the Republicans gave to the rich. The Republican Congress rejected that amendment and insisted on borrowing the money. In short, never acknowledge the charge, but claim credit for doing the right thing.

Bill Clinton benefited from personalizing the 1992 campaign because people related to him more than to the aloof, awkward President Bush. The context of this campaign is that people are in a bad mood and they are inclined to blame the Bush Administration. Kerry can reinforce this public disposition by staying on the offensive, pledging to do what the administration has not done, and not to do what they have done.

Voters want somebody to tell them that things do not have to be this bad, that we can again have a robust economy and a government that serves its people. The best way to do this is to reach back to the 1990s and remind people that they are always better off under Democratic leadership. The more voters perceive the election as a contest between Democratic and Republican priorities, rather than just between two individuals, the better the chance for a real Democratic tidal wave.

# OUR REPUBLICAN FRIENDS

*March 30, 2004*

Everyone, even the Bush strategists, is impressed by the
extent of unity and motivation among the various components of the Democratic Party this year. Last week, Howard
Dean and Joe Lieberman, who could both be divisive influ-
ences from opposing ends of the spectrum, formally
endorsed John Kerry. Interestingly, it was the voters, not the
leaders, who brought this about. They sent a clear message
in the primaries that they did not want Democratic feuding
to facilitate a reelection of George W. Bush.

What a difference this could have made in the low-
turnout 2002 congressional elections. Despite the opportunity created by job losses, Democrats in 2002 floundered in
search of a message and retreated in the face of Bush's
offensive in the war on terror. The Republican base was unified and motivated while Democratic voters were confused
and discouraged.

Motivating the party's base and pulling together has
been step number one in the quest to win back the White
House and Congress. Step number two is attracting independent voters. The usual strategy for this, encouraged by
the Democratic Leadership Council, is to try to blunt the
party's perceived vulnerabilities by moving closer to the
Republican positions on issues like taxes, national security,
and crime. This strategy overlooks the fact that a majority of
independent voters actually lean Democratic, and that many

of the rest are virtual nonvoters. The experience of the primary season revealed that millions of independent voters are listening for the same thing that Democrats are, a coherent message that gives them a reason to vote Democratic.

Democrats and independents can probably deliver the White House to John Kerry, but can they deliver the Congress? Are we condemned to decades of a closely divided government that can never produce rational solutions to national problems? To begin work on a truly progressive agenda, do we, ironically, need some support from Republican voters?

I play tennis with a large group of older citizens. Of the Republicans in the collection, a few have declared their intention to break ranks and vote against George Bush. The rest have stopped defending him. My sister, a lifelong Republican, has changed her registration to Democratic. My cousin, a retired schoolteacher in rural Pennsylvania, is experiencing doubts for perhaps the first time in her life. Millions of Republicans will march over the cliff with Bush, of course, but many others are troubled and confused by what their party has done in the past three years.

In my book, I wrote a chapter called, "Whatever Happened to Liberal Republicans?" The Republican Party once included a substantial number of leaders who treated public service as a calling, and who supported public education, fiscal responsibility, corporate citizenship, civil rights, and social security. They were open to compromise and rational problem-solving in the legislative process. That liberal wing was driven out of the Republican Party by the strident conservatives who rallied behind Barry Goldwater, Ronald Reagan, and Newt Gingrich, but many traditional Republican voters still share those moderate views.

Is it possible to appeal to these Republicans without sacrificing the clarity of the Democratic message? I think it is, but not by parroting Republican rhetoric. As Harry Truman said, given a choice between a real Republican and a phony one, voters will choose the real one. The fundamental principle to be remembered is that the Democratic message has potentially broad appeal if communicated properly, while the Republican message has a potentially narrow appeal if properly exposed.

Many people vote Republican because of family and geographic tradition. In many rural areas and smaller communities, it is taken for granted that respectable people vote Republican. These voters are not truly represented by the wealthy power brokers and cultural extremists who have taken control of the modern Republican Party. In 1964, Hubert Humphrey gave a ringing speech at the Democratic National Convention in which he contrasted moderate Republican views with those of Barry Goldwater. The Republican drive to cut taxes for the wealthy at the expense of everything else, abandoning the traditional concern with fiscal responsibility, presents an opportunity to spell out how the current leadership has strayed from the views of its traditional voters.

Which party has truly served the middle class? The average rate of inflation and the average rate of business failures have been lower under Democratic administrations. Investment returns have been higher under Democrats. The Democratic Party has been responsible for the student financial aid that has been the backbone of higher education. It has supported Social Security and Medicare, which have relieved so many families from the need to support elderly parents. As Democrats, we know all of this by heart, but we do not seem to see a need to remind the voters.

Working class families who were lured away from their Democratic traditions by the Republicans' exploitation of cultural issues have suffered hardship or anxiety in the Bush economy. They are discontented, and many would vote Democratic this year if the party articulated their feelings and gave them reasons to return. Giving tax cuts to the rich does not create jobs in the U.S. It just takes money out of circulation and parks it in the bank accounts of people who do not need it. Working Americans were better off under President Clinton, and have always been better off under Democratic leadership. Numbers are readily available to show this. The so-called Reagan Democrats would nod their heads at this argument.

Democrats have a great opportunity in 2004. A Republican president and Congress have made a mess of everything they have touched, and voters of varied backgrounds are listening for an alternative. Running hundreds of personality campaigns will waste the opportunity. The Democratic approach to government makes sense. History supports it. All it needs is a voice, one that will give voters reasons to do more than just rid the country of a dangerous president.

# LOOKING INWARD

*April 13, 2004*

"We swear to God, we are not afraid to die. We are going to heaven."

The words were spoken by a masked man waving his gun into a video camera, one of the captors of an American hostage in Iraq. Of all the things about Muslims that Americans find difficult to understand, suicide missions are the most disturbing. We forget that in 1945, Japanese teenagers learned how to take off in airplanes but not to land. Steeped in the Shinto doctrine that dying for the emperor would guarantee a life in paradise, they created temporary havoc for the American Navy by flying bomb-laden planes into ships.

Do these people truly not fear death? No, of course they fear death, as do most people. Suicide bombers probably fear death more than most people do, or at least they have been thoroughly imbued with the general fear on which their religion depends for its grip. Actually, what they really fear is the uncertainty of their status after death. Their religious teachers have terrified them with this uncertainty, so much that they are willing to sacrifice the life they have for the one they imagine.

Christianity has a history of martyrdom as well, and it has often been the key to sainthood. But Christian martyrs have usually been persecuted for their faith, victims of violence rather than perpetrators. Are Christianity and its Judaic ancestor therefore more rational, civilized, and peaceful religions?

If fact, a case could be made that no religion has been more violent and aggressive than Christianity. No, we should qualify that. The roots of Christianity, the teachings of Jesus, were a message of tolerance, humility, compassion, unselfishness, and the personal nature of faith. For many Christians, those ideals are standards to reach for in the conduct of their lives. But for many others, including many who have assumed power in the various institutions and sects of Christianity, a fundamental characteristic of the religion has been the obligation to spread the faith.

While the Islamic doctrine of Jihad has called on the faithful to defend their religious culture with violence if necessary, Christian church hierarchies have urged their followers to take the battle of truth into the lands and lives of others. Crusading European armies who invaded the Near East in medieval times converted Muslims at swordpoint. Spanish armies brought along priests to give the natives of North and South America a choice between Christianity and slavery, if the choice was convenient. Inquisitions and massacres in Europe tried to enforce Catholic orthodoxy on reformist sects. Missionaries have sought out villagers is every corner of the world to save their souls, sometimes followed my military force to punish ungrateful natives.

Why does Christianity, or more appropriately people acting in the name of Christianity, have this messianic compulsion? It seems to be the form taken by the same preoccupation with salvation that motivated the Kamikaze and 9/11 hijackers. Perhaps because Christianity is a western religion, suicide is not considered a noble sacrifice. Violence itself is not condoned unless it is unavoidable. Unfortunately, the definition of unavoidable has not been rigorous. It did not protect heretics during the many centuries that they were viewed as a threat to the power of Christian institutions. It has not protected the staff of abortion clinics from people seeking salvation through terrorism. It has not protected American teenagers sent into a dubious battle or Iraqi civilians who find themselves too close to the targets of American firepower. As Bob Dylan said, "You don't count the dead when God's on your side."

Today, we wonder why much of the Iraqi population refuses to accept our protestations of good intentions, our role as liberators and benefactors. We wonder why the clerical leaders of Islam do not educate young Muslims about the evils of violence, convincing them that carrying out a suicide bombing is the surest path to Hell instead of Heaven. Maybe we should ask ourselves how often a priest or pastor takes the pulpit to preach humility about our own beliefs and respect for the religious faiths of others. It is much more likely that the congregation will be asked to pray for those around the world who have not had the good fortune of accepting Christ as their savior. Protestant ministers in particular will likely urge their listeners to miss no opportunity to witness on behalf of the Christian answer.

Jesus said to his disciples that he would make them fishers of men. Judging from his own life, he apparently meant that he would show them how to set an example that would radiate through society and move it toward a more humane existence. In this respect, he was consistent with Buddha, Confucius, Gandhi, Martin Luther King, and Mother Teresa. In the hands of men, however, Christianity has too often interpreted that invitation as a mission to propagate its version of truth.

The most difficult thing in life is to see yourself as others see you. It has been especially difficult for Westerners and Americans in particular. Even when we are acting benevolently, we assume an air of superiority that stems partly from our economic success but also from our conviction that we represent religious truth. Today, we find ourselves in a dangerous, frustrating, puzzling, and depressing conflict. The way out of it is far from clear, and it is difficult to think about long-term solutions when the present is so debilitating. But we must begin a process that will progressively diminish the sources of this conflict over several decades.

The teachings of Jesus are a remarkable foundation for leading a life of self-appreciation and appreciation of others. The basic documents of American democracy are a remarkable foundation for coexistence in a peaceful community. The mixture of public and private responsibility that has evolved in the United States is a remarkable foundation for progress and prosperity. When Americans practice these examples rather than preaching them, they exercise a powerful attraction to people of all cultural backgrounds. Unfortunately, humility is not considered a virtue in American politics; bravado is the coin of the realm. George Bush repeatedly casts complex issues in simple terms of right and wrong, good and evil. His bravado plays well with much of the American public. It plays poorly in the rest of the world, especially in the Muslim world.

# WARNINGS FROM THE PAST

*April 15, 2004*

A politically balanced commission is currently engaged in a
game of cat and mouse with politically balanced witnesses in
what appears to be a fruitless exercise to determine whether
the Bush Administration failed to heed warnings of an
impending terrorist attack. The conclusion is bound to be
inconclusive. Were the warnings specific and unambiguous?
No. Was the administration on high alert to the danger? No.
Was anyone else tuned in during that summer of 2001? No,
except maybe for Richard Clarke and his counter-terror col-
leagues, who had been tuned in for several years without
knowing exactly what to expect. Only the most cynical
opponents of Bush will attempt to hang responsibility for
9/11 on him. He was no more asleep at the wheel than the
rest of us.

More damning was his cavalier dismissal or ignorance of
warnings about the invasion and occupation of Iraq. Some
of the warnings were specific and unambiguous. General
Zinni of the Marines and Joint Chiefs Chairman Shinseki
both warned that the occupation force would have to be
much larger than the invasion force, at least twice what it is
now. Zinni recommended using the Iraqi Army, purged of
Saddam loyalists, to maintain order and avoid a period of
lawlessness. Democrats in Congress, including John Kerry,
warned that going into Iraq without United Nations
approval and help would undermine our claims of good

intentions. We would be seen as an invading and occupying army rather than a participant in an international police action.

Donald Rumsfeld and Paul Wolfowitz dismissed all these warnings with a wave of the hand. The Iraqi people would be so grateful that they would immediately set to work building a democratic model for the Muslim world, using growing oil revenues to assume the financial burden. Not only did we not need more than 130,000 troops, we would begin bringing those home by the summer of 2004.

The less obvious but nonetheless pertinent warnings were found in the history of U.S. involvement in Vietnam. A well-worn proverb says that those who ignore history are condemned to repeat it. None of the major players in the Bush Administration served in Vietnam, and there is nothing in any of their public statements to suggest that they ever seriously studied that national nightmare. Had they done so, they might have anticipated the frustration that American troops are now feeling in Iraq.

The Bush people seem to have used postwar Germany and Japan as their models for occupying a country. The people of those countries were not grateful to us for their liberation, but they were exhausted by war and devastating bombing. In Japan, the emperor made the decision to surrender and instructed his followers to cooperate. We never had to contend with an insurrection, mass demonstrations, or the threat of civil war. In Vietnam, we confronted an enemy that moved seamlessly in and out of the population. We employed our military doctrine, which is to use our firepower to inflict damage on the enemy and accept the inevitability of some mistakes and civilian casualties. When at least some of the population is supporting the guerillas, it actually becomes impossible to distinguish between military and civilian casualties. We could not identify friend from foe, and we sometimes lashed out in desperation.

An occupying power is rarely seen as benevolent, but if it suppresses lawlessness and allows people to go about their business, it will at least achieve acquiescence. We were never able to achieve this in rural Vietnam, where the Vietcong meted out their punishments by night. Eventually, the Tet Offensive showed that we could not assure security in the cities either. Guerilla forces rarely attempt to win battles, except for the last one. Their tactical goal is to prevent peace, and they can accomplish a lot with relatively little fire-power. The Vietnamese population increasingly blamed the Americans for the misery of their country, despite the billions we spent there. The Americans were intruders whose presence just perpetuated the war.

There was, of course, a minority of Vietnamese who were dependent on us for their livelihood and their lives. In Iraq, ironically, this minority is probably the Sunnis, who had done relatively well in the secular regime imposed by Saddam. They are certainly in a quandary, bitter at the Americans for destroying their control, but fearful of the fundamentalist Shiite majority if the Americans leave. The Bush Administration has blamed the Sunnis for much of the resistance, but this is an oversimplification. It is more likely that some of the Sunnis are gathering their strength for an eventual showdown with the Ayatollahs.

One of the major questions in the minds of a people subject to occupation is how long the occupiers will stay. When massive numbers of American troops began arriving in Vietnam, there was a period when the Vietnamese people weighed the situation and many threw in their lot with the westerners. Even before Tet, however, it was becoming clear that American forces could not impose their will, and that cooperation with them would eventually carry a heavy price. No one wants to be on the wrong side when the day of judgement comes, so the people increasingly measure their association with the occupiers and conceal their support of the resistance.

Listening to President Bush at his rare press conference, I was struck by how much his rhetoric echoed that of Lyndon Johnson. It was not just that Johnson grasped for good news and denied the bad, or that he blamed sinister forces for frustrating the will of the majority. It was that once a combat force was committed in 1965, the issue was no longer the potential threat posed by North Vietnam. The issue was the credibility of American power and American resolve to finish what we start. We are there now in Iraq, now that we have been challenged by a hostile force.

Maybe we will be lucky, and the transfer of authority will settle the country long enough for us to get out or get the United Nations in. But I fear not. For eight years, we fought in Vietnam for our credibility. We left only when we accepted defeat and negotiated a phony truce. It's strange, the world never held that against us.

# THOSE DARN POLLS

*April 21, 2004*

Just when everything seemed to be going his way, several polls showed John Kerry slipping behind George Bush and losing some public confidence. Of course, no one should panic. The polls have been jumping around and probably will continue to do so. Moreover, not all the polls have Bush ahead. Finally, the votes that Ralph Nader is siphoning off do not tell us whether he will be on the ballot in the battleground states.

Nonetheless, the little turn of events has to be somewhat unsettling. It comes on the heels of an nearly unbroken run of bad news for Bush: Richard Clarke's charges that he has mismanaged the war on terrorism, an alarming rise in violence in Iraq that has sent American casualties spiraling upward, and an unrelenting rise in gasoline prices. Bush is beginning to resemble the "teflon president" Ronald Reagan in his ability to escape blame for his mistakes.

What is going on here? We might begin by remembering Oscar Wilde's comment, "The only thing worse than being talked about is not being talked about." For months, Bush was in the shadows while the Democrats sorted out their candidates and Iraq smoldered but did not burn. Recently, the news has put the president back on center stage, reluctant as he may be. People are tuned in to see what he will say about all this, how he stands up to it. What he has done is come out fighting, admitting no mistakes, casting issues in black and white, rallying his troops. This is his style, his instinct. However much some of us may despise it and label it "stubborn," at least part of the public is reassured. In the face of a violent challenge, Bush is seen as a strong leader.

Bush will continue this kind of posturing through November, even if he concedes power to the United Nations to avert disaster in Iraq. It will be the cornerstone of his appeal, along with a continuing barrage of advertising that paints Kerry as the opposite: indecisive, unclear, uncertain. It is a formidable strategy and Democrats should not underestimate Bush's ability to pull it off. It can be countered, however.

Since a key part of Bush's strategy is to drive up Kerry's negatives, it is tempting to reply in kind. In effect, you could try to convince people to vote against Bush rather than for Kerry. The problem with this approach is that the election becomes a referendum on Bush's presidency, and the public will tune in to see how he defends himself. Some Democrats are looking forward to this, but they should beware of wishful thinking. Bush has no qualms about redefining history and portraying the present situation with little regard for reality. He knows that if you lie with conviction, many people will believe you. If you give him the pulpit, he will cast the debate on his terms.

Up to a point, the election will inevitably be a referendum on Bush, and Democrats must try to turn it against him. But this has to be done with finesse. Rather than just accusing Bush of favoritism to the rich, Kerry can say again and again, "Tax cuts for the rich just drive up our national debt and do not create jobs." Rather than accusing Bush of misleading the country, Kerry can say, "We will not rush into war when I am president, but if we must use force, we will do it with broad international support.and I will tell the

American people the truth." Instead of criticizing the Medicare drug bill, Kerry can say, "I will put the interests of senior citizens above those of the big drug companies." In short, you can get a negative without sounding too personal and get a positive in the same sentence.

Working on Bush's obvious negatives can be only part of a successful strategy, however. A lot of people want to vote against Bush, probably a majority. What they are looking for is a rationale for doing so. John Kerry, a very intelligent, sincere, and thoughtful man, has not inspired a following yet, and he may not do so. He has not been able to shed his aloof, intellectual style, open shirt or not. He is not, frankly, as comfortable and quick with a quip as Bush is. Kerry does have to reassure people and work on his positives, but personal attributes alone are not going to turn this election against the incumbent.

"It's the economy, stupid," was the watchword of the 1992 campaign. "It's the Republican economy," should be the watchword in 2004. I feel like I have said this until I'm blue in the face. Democratic government versus Republican government is a stronger card than Kerry versus Bush. People are feeling insecure in their jobs and their neighborhoods, and this is always true under Republican government. People are paying higher fees and property taxes to make up for the huge federal budget deficit, and this is always true under Republican government. People have seen the value of their investments decline, and this is always true under Republican government. Our natural environment is in danger, and this is always true under Republican government.

When Democrats take control of the government, consumer, investor, and business confidence always go up. Jobs are created, unemployment declines, the stock market does better, business failures go down, bankruptcies go down, crime rates go down. The data show this unmistakably.

Instead of taking money out of circulation through tax cuts for the rich, Democrats get money into the hands of working families and the economy takes off. Everybody, even the wealthy, does better. It's not rocket science.

The rationale is there, it's just waiting for a voice. Democrats missed a golden opportunity to tell their story in 2000, but it's not too late. Kerry has a credible position on Iraq and the war against terrorism. He can spell out his approach in five minutes and move on to the economy. Instead of trying to outbid Bush with new tax cut proposals, he should level with people. A Democratic congress and president will rescind the Bush tax cuts for the wealthy and get the federal budget under control. They will raise the minimum wage and get money into the economy with public works and aid to the states. They will require that American workers be used for all domestic services paid for with federal funds.

The polls will bounce around from now to November, and they will not be a good predictor of who will actually vote. What is crucial is what voters are thinking in the final week. Will the Democrats have given them reasons to vote Democratic, or will we just pay our nickel and take our chances?

# PENETRATING THE MIST

*May 2, 2004*

The American broadcast press has been accused of liberal bias and conservative bias, but nobody has ever accused it of having sophisticated insight. Still, its current portrayal of the relative positions of President Bush and John Kerry on the dilemma of Iraq has attained a new level of superficiality. The standard line heard on "election analysis" segments is that the two men have reached a basic consensus on our need to "stay the course" while soliciting help from the United Nations and NATO allies to lessen the burden on American troops. They have, according to some analysts, moved toward each other.

As someone who follows the election campaign closely enough to understand fundamental differences, I wonder about the futility of trying to follow it through the filter of the broadcast press. To me, the differences are crystal clear. Kerry would not have committed U.S. troops and resources to an invasion of Iraq without a Security Council or NATO decision that Iraq was a source of terrorism or an imminent threat to become one. He would have pursued terrorist organizations through international cooperation and covert actions, and today we would have much more to show for our efforts.

Given the Bush Administration's decision to destroy Iraq's government and the breakdown of order that has followed, Kerry must come to grips with a situation that was

85

not of his own making. He has focused on the potential consequences of allowing Iraq to descend into civil war. Not only would the country become a likely haven for Al Queda, it could fall under control of Islamist radicals and become another Afghanistan. The chances of major destabilization in the Arab world would be very real.

Kerry has thus taken the position that we must finish what we started, but his approach to doing so is materially different from that of Bush. While Bush has reluctantly paid lip service to the need for help from the UN and NATO, Kerry would do what is necessary: seek a collective decision on how to proceed. Unless we treat our allies and the Secretary General as equals, we will get no help in the vital step of turning an American occupation into an international peacekeeping operation. We cannot snub other nations one moment and lecture them the next if we want their participation, which we desperately need.

All of this is clear to me and should be to the well-paid press. If we cannot expect much from the press, however, maybe we should expect more from Kerry. I feel certain I have accurately characterized his position, but who has actually heard him put it that way? Who has heard him put aside the pieties and cautiously constructed sentences and semantic detours and said, "Look, here's the difference between him and me?" The Bush campaign is out to characature John Kerry just like the Bush Sr. campaign did to Michael Dukakis in 1988. So far, he is making it easy for them.

It is not easy for a leopard to change his spots. Al Gore tried to adopt a warmer personality and could not. Kerry has tried, but many voters still perceive him as aloof, austere, even arrogant. Moreover, the mood of the country is less conducive to lightheartedness than it was in 2000. What is John Kerry to do, then?

Voters may not wait to shake his hand like they did for

John Kennedy and Bill Clinton, but they will vote for him if they know what to expect from a Kerry presidency. A majority does not want four more years of George Bush, and they want to know if they have another choice. Kerry offers a choice, a different set of priorities and policies with the prospect of a return to peace and prosperity. The question is whether the voters will know this. It would be a tragedy if a majority decided that better the devil you know than the one you don't.

Kerry needs to be straightforward in explaining things he has done and those he will do. He needs to be succinct. The press is constantly looking for soundbites, and Kerry could craft some that capsulize his reasoning. Up to now, he has taken so long to make his points that he sounds fragmented and out of context. If he has taken logical positions in the past and has logical positions for the future, they can be conveyed efficiently so the press can use them.

Kerry could also make a better impression if he tried to sound more thoughtful and less scripted. He always seems in a hurry, starting new sentences before his audience digests the previous one. It is better to help the audience think along with you. For example, "If you want to create jobs, you have to get money circulating in the economy. Tax cuts for the rich don't do that." Kerry could also invoke what people are telling him around the country. He could sound like he's listening as well as giving speeches. He could ask whether President Bush really knows what is happening to people.

With events moving so fast, Iraq may have already escaped our control by November. We may have already grasped for a Nixon-Kissinger sleight of hand to cover our disengagement. If Iraq is still festering, it will be a huge albatross around Bush's neck. For Kerry to benefit from this, however, he must be candid about the alternative approach he offers. He must have articulated his case in a way that even the broadcast press can understand. This is no time for clouding differences, the stakes for the country are too high. We are veering dangerously off course in both foreign and domestic policy and we need to see our way back.

# SHOCK AND DISBELIEF

*May 13, 2004*

In the past week, we have heard the president and Secretary of Defense express shock and disbelief at the pictures of humiliating and intimidating treatment of Iraqi prisoners by American military police. President Bush came close to apologizing to the Iraqi people but mostly tried to convince them that the actions of a handful of soldiers did not represent the values and intentions of America. Bush also let it be known that he had chastised Secretary Rumsfeld for keeping him in the dark about what was going on.

Listening to the pleas of our commanders-in-chief, I was reminded again that these two men who control the power to pulverize the world seem to know so little about war. Of course, it is possible that Bush and Rumsfeld were well aware that abusive techniques were being used to extract information. If so, their protestations of ignorance are as cynical as Richard Nixon's denials of the Watergate cover-up.

I doubt that many people who have been in combat were shocked by what they saw. Nothing in human experience is truly comparable to combat. While officers may worry about achieving their assigned objectives and advancing their careers, enlisted men are preoccupied with survival, their own and their comrades'. Danger can come from anywhere; paranoia becomes a virtue. There is a constant temptation to shoot first and ask questions later, leading to many of the incidents of soldiers being killed by friendly fire.

However, most people are not natural-born killers. They have been taught from childhood to value human life, an admonition reinforced by the legal system. To assume the necessary role of reliable killers, soldiers must learn to dehumanize the enemy. They are trained for this and absorb it quickly under fire. In World War II, we did not fight people from Japan and Germany, we fought Nips, Japs, Krauts, and Jerries. In Vietnam, we fought VC, NVA, and gooks, a term that came to cover most Vietnamese.

Having dehumanized the enemy when he is fighting, it is not easy to humanize him when he is powerless. Although treatment of German prisoners in Europe was generally good, there were numerous incidents of random executions, mostly out of revenge. In the Pacific, incidents where wounded Japanese turned themselves into human booby traps led to a practice of shooting them and leaving them lay. Early in the Korean War, American troops trying to stabilize their lines massacred hundreds of refugees fleeing North Korean forces. In Vietnam, one interrogation tactic was to take some VC for a helicopter ride, throw one out, and then question the rest.

These are the things that happen during a war. The Bush campaign has tried to discredit John Kerry by, among other things, criticizing his 1971 testimony about atrocities in Vietnam. They would have done better to reflect on what he said. He tried to tell the Senate that political decisions had put American troops in an impossible situation, where they were supposed to fight a war and witness for democracy at the same time. As in Iraq, it was difficult in Vietnam to sort out the enemy from the people we were supposed to help. Exasperation at the dilemma led to indiscriminate killing, culminating in the massacre at My Lai.

During the 2000 campaign, George Bush argued that

American forces should not be used for "nation building," but rather reserved for genuine threats to our security. The implied criticism of the Clinton Administration's interventions in Haiti and Yugoslavia was off base, since those were limited operations intended mainly to separate warring factions. It is doubtful that Bush even understood what he was talking about, but he should have listened to himself. Using the military to overthrow a dictatorship and build a democratic society is like using a sledgehammer to repair a computer.

American military forces are remarkably well prepared for their primary purpose, defeating an enemy force in the air, on the ground, and at sea. Given a purely military scenario, they can prevail anywhere in the world. They are ill suited, however, for political missions that require restraint, sensitivity, and diplomacy. That Bush, Rumsfeld, and Wolfowitz expected American troops to transition overnight from relentless fighters to ambassadors for democracy betrays a remarkable degree of naivete and historical ignorance.

Predictably, the Pentagon and White House have set out to isolate the scandal at the lowest possible level. The "few bad apples," however, were following instructions from intelligence officers and private intelligence contractors. These, in turn, were responding to pressures from Central Command, which was trying to assure the Secretary of Defense that "pacification" was succeeding. Rumsfeld, for his part, was trying desperately to salvage the Iraq gamble in order to salvage Bush's reelection. Is there any wonder that the National Guard troops pressed into service as prison guards, finding themselves hated and under daily mortar attacks, took it out on Iraqi prisoners?

The Nixon Administration tried to contain the Watergate scandal by paying the burglars to take the fall.

When that did not work, they tried to sacrifice John Dean, then John Mitchell, then John Ehrlichman. When there were no more Johns, Nixon's Chief of Staff Bob Haldeman walked the plank. Finally, there was no one left but Nixon himself.

Harry Truman had a sign on his desk that read, "The buck stops here." Bush should have one that says, "The buck stops somewhere else." This buck, however, may keep climbing.

# AMERICA CAN RECOVER

*May 18, 2004*

The incredible advances in communications technology
mean that stories and pictures circulate at breakneck speed
and spread to every corner of the globe. So it did not take
long for the photos of American guards degrading Iraqi
prisoners to become the main topic of conversation just
about everywhere. By all accounts, America's reputation has
sunk to historic lows, jeopardizing what little is left of
President Bush's "Coalition of the Willing" that joined us in
Iraq.

   Americans traveling abroad are treated not so much
with hostility as bewilderment. People around the world are
wondering how this came to pass, how a country that
enjoyed widespread admiration at the end of the 20th century and universal sympathy after the 9/11 attacks could have
squandered it all in an exhibition of arrogance, boorishness,
and naivete. The world is wondering, too, what would be the
consequence of these attitudes continuing after the
November election.

   Many Americans are despairing of this turn of events
and worrying that long-term damage has been done to our
position in world affairs. This is not necessarily true. Those
of us who traveled abroad during the Vietnam War can
remember the contempt in which the Johnson and Nixon
Administrations were held and the astonishment that political assassinations were determining the course of American

politics.

By the time we called it quits in Vietnam, American prestige in the world was at rock bottom. It would wax and wane in the future, however, rising during the Carter Administration, falling with the dollar under Reagan, then recovering under the elder Bush and Bill Clinton before the current disaster. It is instructive to examine the characteristics of American leadership during these periods.

Jimmy Carter brought an appreciation of the complexities of international relations and a particular sympathy for the peoples of Africa. He pressed the white minority government of South Africa to end apartheid and share power with the native majority. He insisted that Israel negotiate with Egypt and mediated a settlement of their long-standing conflict. Carter showed a patience and persistence in seeking diplomatic solutions that was respected in most of the world. It would have succeeded in resolving the Iran hostage crisis as well, but time ran out. The virtues that served him well in the world community were turned against him in the 1980 election campaign.

George Bush Sr. had served as Ambassador to the United Nations and knew the importance of working in concert with our allies and other major countries in resolving international crises. When Iraq invaded Kuwait, Bush tried economic sanctions long enough to satisfy the Security Council and achieve the broad support needed to expel Iraqi forces. Bush also actively pursued agreements to remove trade barriers, a policy that held promise for diminishing cultural differences among nations.

Bill Clinton built on his predecessor's policies of free trade and multilateralism, picking up as well President Carter's example of mediation. Clinton achieved another step toward peace in Palestine, oversaw a negotiated truce in Northern Ireland, and joined NATO efforts to pacify the civil conflicts in the former Yugoslavia. Perhaps more importantly, his domestic policies enabled the U.S. economy to display its dynamism, attracting worldwide admiration. Erudite and articulate, Clinton was warmly greeted wherever he traveled. By the end of his term, America's Vietnam folly was forgotten.

Although world opinion of the U.S. did not fall as much under Reagan as it has under the younger Bush, there were similarities in the underlying causes. Both men were parochial in their view of the world and unaccustomed to conversing with foreign leaders. They compensated by boasting about the virtues and capabilities of America as the natural leader of the world. Both overestimated threats well beyond the level that seemed realistic to our NATO allies: the Soviet Union in Reagan's case, Iraq under Bush. Both flexed American military power to an extent that unsettled the Europeans. Both gave unreserved support to Israel and minimal importance to the peace process.

Despite the bluster, however, other nations perceived a fundamental weakening of the American economy under the Reagan and Bush Administrations, characterized by soaring national debt and trade deficits and a devaluation of the dollar. The sale of American assets to the Japanese and Saudis under Reagan and to the Europeans under Bush have been one consequence of this economic weakness.

The decline of America's standing in the world need not be permanent. There remains a large reservoir of potential goodwill toward the U.S., based on our natural wealth, the casual good-natured inclinations of our people, and most of all our history of freedom and diversity. Much of the world wants to admire America, almost like a son wants to admire his father. When we entrust our government to men like Nixon, Reagan, and George W. Bush, we betray the faith that somehow America will show the way to a better world.

We can begin the process of rebuilding by promising a change in November. We can pledge ourselves to a policy of international dialogue and cooperation, of seeking consensus among the major powers rather than lecturing them. We can put our economic house in order by rescinding the reckless tax cuts than have undermined our prosperity and weakened the dollar. We can rejoin international efforts to reduce oil consumption and protect the environment. We can regain our progressive image by properly funding education and setting out to resolve our health care deficiency once and for all.

John Kerry and the Democrats can help get America back on track by spelling out the alternatives they offer to the policies and attitudes of the Bush Administration. All of us, citizens of the United States and citizens of the world, can start looking forward to a better day. This is what the majority wants to hear. This is what will nullify the barrage of attack advertising from the Bush warchest.

# THE ROOT OF ALL EVIL

*May 30, 2004*

In recent days, John Kerry flirted with a novel idea before thankfully relegating it to the trash bin. Because of a curious provision in the presidential campaign financing act, Kerry's nomination in late July will be treated as the official start of his campaign, subjecting him to the $75 million spending limit imposed on candidates who accept public funds. President Bush, in contrast, can continue unlimited spending until the Republican convention five weeks later. Some clever fool in the Kerry camp suggested, therefore, that he delay his acceptance of the Democratic nomination until well after the convention. Such a ruse would have presented the Republicans with a public relations bonanza.

Kerry may find another way to compensate for the Republican scheduling coup, but the incident shows once again the absurdity of campaign financing laws in the United States. The U.S. is the only democracy in the world that allows a free-for-all in the funding of campaigns for public office. Much ballyhooed attempts to control it, like McCain-Feingold and the Watergate-era legislation, have only led to more inventiveness in how money is raised and spent. Visualize a large inflated doll that is weighted at the bottom so it will bounce back up whenever it is knocked over.

Money is the lifeblood of American politics. The Bush campaign will directly spend well over $300 million on his reelection, and Kerry will probably spend over $200 million.

When all the "independent" organizations have chipped in with their "issue advertising" and voter mobilization efforts, the 2004 presidential campaign will have probably cost over $1 billion. And that is just the beginning. The 33 senate and 435 house campaigns could easily add $500 million. Thousands more candidates will try to be heard in campaigns for governor, attorney general, secretary of state, state legislatures, and so on. For the voters, this will become a blur by October.

A well-qualified citizen tempted to run for office faces the unpleasant prospect of going hat-in-hand to friends, family, strangers, and, most importantly, organized groups. Should one survive this and win a seat in Congress or a state assembly, he or she must begin immediately to raise money for reelection two years later. U.S. Senate campaigns have become so expensive that even a six-year term does not relieve incumbents from the continuous quest for donations. In this environment, it is no wonder that the best and brightest among us pass up the calling of elected representative.

Legislators from both parties, but Republicans probably more than Democrats, feel great pressure to accommodate the groups that made their election possible. We hear a lot about this at the national level, but it is even more pervasive in state legislatures. Whether it is realtors, developers, plumbers, electricians, attorneys, or an assortment of other groups active in local economies, they have carefully lined up the support needed for laws that tilt the balance in their favor and against consumers. The American media often comments on the corruption of politics in countries of Asia, Africa, and Latin America. The fact is that most legislation in the U.S. is initially written be interested groups who then use campaign contributions to get what they want or prevent what they do not want.

The Supreme Court has given campaign contributions the constitutional status of free speech, subject only to "reasonable" restrictions. It has allowed limitations on individual contributions, currently $2,000, and has tolerated the prohibition of direct contributions from corporations. The presidential spending limit passes muster only because it is optional: both candidates and taxpayers can opt out of it. In 2000, George W. Bush became the first candidate to decline public funding and go it alone. It is possible that both candidates will do so this year, thus nullifying the country's one hesitant step to provide an alternative to the money chase in national elections.

In the late 1990's, four states adopted public financing programs for state elections. Maine, Arizona, and Massachusetts did so by citizen initiative, while Vermont's legislature acted. Reform has also moved forward in New Mexico and North Carolina. Because state supreme courts have generally tolerated no restrictions on private financing, these programs had to be voluntary for candidates. If they accepted public funds, they had to forgo private contributions and personal spending. A key problem, therefore, was the possibility that a participating candidate might be financially overwhelmed by a nonparticipating opponent. Provision was made, therefore, to increase public funds during the campaign if spending by the two candidates was becoming disparate. However, since much of the spending occurs in the final month and is not reported until just before the election, the effectiveness of these provisions was in doubt. Further concerns arose from the demands of independent and minor party candidates.

Notwithstanding the complications and the Massachusetts legislature's repeal of the act in that state, these initiatives were enormous steps in the right direction. An able candidate who was unable or unwilling to raise much money could now enter a primary and look forward to having the means to run a serious campaign. Moreover, the public in these states showed its understanding of the issue and its willingness to support a major change. Republican politicians take great pleasure in asserting sarcastically that people do not want their tax money used for political campaigns. The fact is that much of the public is willing to substitute tax money for the current corrupt system, which they know allows public policy to be bought and sold.

There is probably no reform that could have a more profound effect on the American political system than adopting an effective system of public financing for legislative campaigns. However, with no opportunity for national citizen initiatives, with so many other things pressing, and with incumbents enjoying the fruits of the current system, its chances of even getting a hearing are remote. Nonetheless, 2003 and 2004 have been interesting years for campaign finance. Howard Dean's campaign revealed the power of the Internet for gathering small contributions. No longer does a candidate have to spend substantial time and money mailing solicitations, then hope they will be opened and read and that someone will take the trouble to write a check and mail it so it can be manually processed and accounted for by campaign staff. Once an email list is compiled, often from visits to the campaign's web site, mass messages can be sent effortlessly. Sympathizers can click to a form, fill out the necessary information for electronic bookkeeping, and use their credit cards to contribute. Almost any size contribution becomes profitable, the more the merrier.

Before we conclude that the Internet is going to revolutionize campaign financing, we must remember that the Iraq invasion provided a powerful motivation for people to dig into their pockets. This kind of grass roots largesse may not be sustainable without such a rallying cry. Moreover, progressives are not the only ones who know how to use the Internet. To some extent, this new facility in tapping small donors may just up the ante for running a campaign. The big donors, who can reimburse family members for their $2,000 checks and round up colleagues in the executive suite, will still be a force in the process.

America has the best democracy money can buy. As a consequence, the wealthiest country in the world has the worst record of any modern democracy in taking rational action to solve its basic social and economic problems. We are the world's primary underachievers, and will continue to be as long as wealth can veto any initiative that threatens privilege. Politicians think the people do not understand this. They are wrong. Give the people a chance and they would do something about it.

# CHILDREN, ECONOMICS, AND POLITICS

*June 4, 2004*

Recent newspaper stories in Atlanta have reported the concerns of the Georgia Division of Child Protective Services about the alarming growth of its caseload over the past year. Caseworkers are not able to give families the attention they deserve and the number of children placed in the holding pattern of foster care has been rising. The many children left in the charge of abusive or negligent parents are like a time bomb - waiting to explode into a major scandal for the division.

That child abuse and neglect are increasing is disheartening but not surprising. It is disheartening because the problem declined consistently during the 1990s. It is not surprising because we are in our fourth year of a weak job market with individual periods of unemployment lasting longer and longer. Prolonged unemployment affects both men and women, but the social and psychological consequences are more pronounced for men because so much of their self-esteem is related to their ability to earn a living and provide for a family. When a man is confronted with prolonged unemployment, he is vulnerable to depression and may begin to resent those who have depended on him. He is more apt to become involved with alcohol or drugs and may be more inclined to violence.

Single men may be tempted to resort to petty crime, especially if they have had previous episodes. Young men in particular are susceptible to seeking income from illegal activities. Crime statistics are gathered at a glacial pace, so trends do not appear immediately. However, anecdotal evidence suggests that property crime and robbery have been increasing for a year or more. Already in 2002, the National Victimization Survey showed an increase in car theft, a leading indicator. This comes after property crime had fallen a stunning 45 percent in the prosperous years of the Clinton Administration.

The statistical connection between the health of the job market and social ills such as crime, alcoholism, domestic violence, and even teenage pregnancy is well established. While unemployment does not cause all of these problems, it clearly aggravates their incidence. The short-term unemployment that occurs in a prosperous economy does not have a great impact because people have a reasonable expectation of returning to work at an acceptable job. In a sluggish economy, however, such hopes are often dashed and the work that is available is often sporadic, at low pay and without benefits. Those with marginal credentials give up the search and are not even counted in official unemployment statistics.

America pays a heavy price for the social dysfunctionality that accompanies high unemployment. We have the highest rate of imprisonment in the world, and the most expensive system of law enforcement and justice. We spend billions, but not nearly enough, taking care of children from broken families and monitoring those in borderline situations. Far too many children grow up without positive role models and without aspirations for success. A high proportion of Americans are victims of crime each year, most of it monetary but some of it violent. All of this crime is intrusive and undermines our feelings of security. Moreover, the unemployment and underemployment of recent years has reached into the middle class, unsettling the sense of well being that had been taken for granted.

Viewed in its total context, the goal of a robust job market should be at the top of government's priority list. President Bush claims it as a priority, but it appears to be more of an afterthought in his quest to lower the tax burden of the wealthy. There is scant evidence that his policies will bring unemployment back down, yet he has persisted in proposing new ways to help his favored class. A generous interpretation of his behavior would be that he does not understand economics; a less generous one would be that he does not care.

Jobs are created when money circulates. The faster it circulates, the more jobs are created. Republicans argue that the more money is put in private hands rather than government, the more it will circulate. Their idea of "private hands," however, has been disproportionately hands that already have plenty of money. Taking money from government and giving it to the wealthy actually slows the pace of circulation. Government spends money quickly because it normally runs a deficit. Moreover, most of the money spent by government goes directly or indirectly into the pockets of low- and middle-income people, in the form of benefits, salaries, or payments to contractors. Some people become rich from government business, it's true, but this is not a lot of money in the greater scheme of things.

The wealthy save a disproportionate amount of their income or invest it in property. During prosperous times, they may invest substantially in the stock market, fueling the buildup of speculative capital. During slack times, however, much of this investment is withdrawn, further aggravating the slowdown. The wealthy also spend a disproportionate share on foreign travel, foreign property, and imported luxury goods, which hardly helps the job market in the U.S.

The progressive income tax, which since the 1930's has been a foundation of public finance in the U.S., has been under sustained attack from conservatives for over twenty years. This is ironic, for the progressive income tax is actually the goose that lays the golden eggs for the wealthy business class. Leave aside for the moment that it is an efficient form of taxation - it goes where the money is. Leave aside the ethical argument that those who have benefited most from our political system should pay a greater share of the cost. The truth is that the progressive income tax is an engine of prosperity precisely because it redistributes wealth from high-income to low- and moderate-income families. Money that would languish is put into circulation and the demand for goods and services drives economic growth. And in the end, it is the wealthy, those who live from profits, who benefit most.

This has been consistently true since government became a major economic player during the Great Depression. The economy has done better under Democratic administrations because the Democrats have tipped the balance of tax and wage policy, however modestly, in favor of working people. When the economy does better, every class of the population does better, and the results show up in the social statistics.

At some point, government could in fact take too much of national income and crowd out too much private activity. We are a long way from that in the United States. Only Turkey has a lower tax burden among industrialized countries. Before we sink to last place and further damage our economic and social balance, let us hope that voters will see the Bush policy for what it is: simple favoritism.

# MYTHOLOGY

*June 13, 2004*

After a week of nonstop tributes and commentary, I hesitate
to add anything to the flood of words about Ronald Reagan.
I have no desire to speak ill of the dead. From all accounts,
Reagan was a very decent and genuine human being. He was
gracious to a fault and made people from all walks of life
feel comfortable. He was a celebrity without pretensions,
acting instead like your favorite uncle. Despite his conservatism, he did not indulge in the bitter partisanship brought
to American government by Newt Gingrich, Dick Armey,
Tom Delay, and the Bushes. Democrats found him hard to
dislike.

Republicans have carefully constructed myths around
Reagan and they missed no opportunity to embellish them
this past week. What better way to distract attention from an
unpopular Republican president than to remind people of
how much they owed to the last popular one? I cannot
blame the Republicans for seizing the opportunity, but their
assertions about Reagan should not be accepted uncritically.

Democrats had a hard time coping with Reagan. They
began by underestimating him, thinking he was a lightweight.
They assumed that Republicans would remember the
Goldwater disaster and would not nominate another western
conservative for president. When he was nominated,
Democrats thought Reagan would expose his extremism
during the campaign and be easy to beat. After he won and

carried a Republican majority to the Senate, some Democrats began overestimating him. Intimidated by his claim that voters had given him a mandate, enough House Democrats acquiesced to allow Reagan his cherished tax cut in 1981.

A number of myths were invoked this week. It was said that Americans were suffering a malaise, and that Reagan restored a sense of optimism and national pride. There is some truth to this. The 1970's had been a difficult passage for the country, beginning with the acceptance of defeat in Vietnam and the first oil embargo that unleashed a wave of hyperinflation. Nixon fell victim to Watergate and the nation struggled with an elusive energy crisis, culminating in a second oil shortage related to the taking of American hostages by Islamic militants in Iran. Jimmy Carter had run for president as an optimist, but became increasingly grim as he tried to wean Americans from their dependence on cheap foreign oil and bring the Iranian government to its senses.

Both the hostage and energy crises soon faded into history, but hardly because of anything Reagan did. The Iranians wanted their assets unfrozen and seemingly ended the affair as a gesture to the new president. Energy prices were already falling as a result of conservation measures, deregulation of natural gas prices by Carter, and the development of new sources in Alaska, Russia, Mexico, and the North Sea. As the price of oil broke, so did overall inflation. Nothing was required of Reagan, nor, for that matter, of interest rate hawk Paul Volcker. Still, Reagan's personality and conviction did lift the spirits of many people. By 1984, he could run for reelection on his "morning in America" ads and a majority nodded in agreement.

A second myth was that voters gave Reagan a mandate to cut taxes and domestic programs and hike defense spending. Public opinion polls never showed any such mandate. Reagan won a personality contest in circumstances that were unfavorable for the incumbent, but only his attack on welfare actually resonated with the public. Resentment toward the poor had accelerated as the middle class suffered hard times in the 1970s, and Reagan had used it as a springboard in California. Whether he understood his own distortions of the issue or not, it was the least admirable facet of his political persona. True to his word, Reagan presided over a decade in which the rich got richer and the poor got poorer.

Faced with the disagreeable fact that the national debt tripled under Reagan, Republicans have argued that he would have balanced the budget if Democrats had let him. However, Reagan never submitted a balanced budget to Congress. His first two budget directors have both written of their frustration that tax cuts and defense spending were given priority over balancing the budget. They acknowledged that projections of future revenue dividends from economic growth were based on wishful thinking. Moreover, for the first six years of Reagan's presidency, every nickel of federal spending was approved by a Republican-controlled Senate.

The favorite Republican myth is that Reagan's defense buildup and strident tone won the Cold War. Since the fall of the Soviet Union, no former Communist leader has confirmed this. The explanation most often given is that the Communist Party was losing its grip because of economic stagnation and the bloody quagmire of its war in Afghanistan. Mikhail Gorbachev tried to salvage the situation by opening up the political process to dissent and the economic system to enterprise, but his reforms just opened the floodgates. The Reagan Administration did provide arms to the mujahadeen rebels in Afghanistan, who later used them to set up the Taliban regime in concert with Osama bin Laden. This policy contributed something to the

Kremlin's loss of control. Whether it contributed more than American rock music is an interesting question.

The notion that America became stronger under Reagan is true only if strength is judged by the percent of national income devoted to the military. The dollar fell so far relative to the yen that Japanese companies went on a buying spree in the U.S. If strength involves a rising standard of living, it was confined in the 1980s to the affluent and to certain parts of the country that benefited from defense spending. The midwestern Rust Belt did poorly, as did the western oil patch. The middle class tread water while the lower class lost ground. This is well documented by former Republican strategist Kevin Phillips in his book, *The Politics of Rich and Poor.*

A critical myth for Republicans is that Reaganomics, cutting taxes on the rich so they will have more to invest, was responsible for a decade of prosperity. In fact, prosperity was spotty under Reagan, and the overall rate of economic growth in the 1980s was the lowest of any decade since the Great Depression. A stock market panic occurred in October 1987, leading to regulation of program trading. Reagan left his successor, the elder George Bush, a deteriorating fiscal situation that blossomed into a full-blown recession. Prosperity returned to the U.S. only when Bill Clinton risked his political future by achieving a modest rollback of Reagan's tax cuts on corporations and high incomes.

Mythology is a powerful weapon in politics. Democrats used it for years to remind people that Franklin Roosevelt pulled us out of the Depression, a half-truth at best. Occasional attempts to revisit some of the myths about Washington, Jefferson, Lincoln, or Teddy Roosevelt generally roll off people's shoulders. We want our leaders to be larger than life. The myths about Reagan are thoroughly partisan, but they are powerful nonetheless. Now that the man is gone, now that the week of mourning is past, Democrats would do well to persistently challenge those myths. The alternative is to play under their shadow.

# FISHING IN TROUBLED WATERS

*June 27, 2004*

The Bush Administration has a tiger by the tail and does not seem to have a clue about how to control it. Islamic extremists from various countries have seized the opportunity created by our destruction of the Iraqi government. They are mounting an escalating campaign of suicide violence against American forces and anyone who cooperates with them. Even more bedeviling is the attitude of much of the Iraqi people, who are either firing rockets and grenades at U.S. forces or complaining that they are not being protected.

It is clear that the American occupation itself is a major source of the violence, yet many Iraqis are preparing for an even more dangerous situation when the occupiers leave. The weapons stashed in mosques, schools, and houses may be used against Americans, but more likely they will be saved for the struggle that Iraqis believe is coming: Sunnis and Kurds against Shiites, or more precisely, against Muslim extremists. The Kurds have enjoyed autonomy under the cover of NATO air forces, and they are wary of joining in a new Iraq. The Sunnis enjoyed privileges and secular freedom under Saddam Hussein, and they fear the designs of radical Shiites on their way of life. Most Iraqis fear the intrusion of Al Qaida and similar terrorist groups who may try to use the country as a base of operations.

There is, therefore, reason to fear that Iraq will become a more dangerous, threatening, and miserable place than it was under Saddam. Such an outcome is an all too familiar theme in American foreign policy. It springs from the historical isolation of the United States and the unwillingness of our elected leaders to learn about the world or to think about it in any terms other than the simplest imperatives of American politics. Too often, we have sallied forth into a fantasy world and been confounded by its behavior.

For years after the breakdown of our World War II alliance with the Soviet Union, we insisted on interpreting conflicts everywhere as part of the death struggle between democracy and communism. Beginning in Greece, wealthy elites and petty dictators on every continent learned the language that would bring arms, and armed force if necessary, to cement their power. This was all presented to the American people as a strategy for containing Soviet Communism and extending the benefits of freedom to peoples who had not known it. Both parties traveled the path, the only difference being that the Democrats believed the fantasy and were constantly frustrated by the cynicism of their proteges in Asia, Africa, and Latin America.

A few Americans tried to warn that we were casting our lot with predatory elements in deep social conflicts that we did not understand, but these voices were drowned out and often punished. Most politicians saw their career opportunities in simplistic expressions of toughness against a supposed Soviet grand design. Like rats following the pied piper, Americans marched into the swamp of Vietnam and paid a fearful price for a lesson in third-world reality.

The Cold War is over now. The Soviet Union has broken down into a collection of more or less democratic countries, struggling with ethnic conflicts and political novelty. For almost three decades, despite the silly bravado of Ronald

Reagan, it seemed like the sobering experience of Vietnam had made Americans more mature in their appreciation of world complexity. Lying in the grass, however, was an assortment of former Reagan and Bush officials, nostalgic cold warriors, Israeli collaborators, oilmen, and defense contractors, all anxious for a new mission. Simple imperialism would not fly, of course, so the American people had to believe in a new and insidious threat.

Saddam Hussein, the delusional, unscrupulous, cocky dictator of Iraq, was the favorite target from the beginning of the Bush Administration. Not only was he sitting on vast reserves of underused oil, he had made no secret of his delight that he had politically outlasted the first President Bush. Saddam, however, was hemmed in by economic sanctions, NATO overflights, and Kurdish autonomy in Northern Iraq. To most Americans he was history, hardly worth the trouble of spying on. Then came September 11, 2001.

The Bush Administration's manipulation of intelligence to convince Americans that Saddam was the principal terrorist threat is now a well-known story. It was not just the public that was misled, however. Bush and his neoconservative junta had allowed Iraqi exiles to lead them down a path that had been traveled before. American power, money, and political guidance would create the conditions in which democratic capitalism would grow as an alternative to evil dictatorship. The Iraqi people had been oppressed, and would gladly become poster children for the American way of life if given the chance.

More than 20 years ago, the Carter Administration facilitated the downfall of the Shah of Iran, believing a liberal western democracy could take the place of the Shah's brutal but westernized dictatorship. Instead, the Ayatollah Khomeini returned from exile and rallied militant Muslims behind his plan for an Islamic theocracy. Human rights in Iran actually fell further from western ideals than they had under the Shah. Moreover, the Ayatollah showed his appreciation by tolerating the militants' occupation of the American Embassy, leading to Carter's defeat in 1980.

In the 1980s, the Reagan Administration viewed with alarm the Soviet intervention to save a Leftist government that was trying to modernize Afghanistan. American arms were channeled through Pakistan to Islamic tribes fighting a guerilla resistance, a war that dragged through the decade and helped undermine the control of the Communist Party in Soviet Union. The Soviets finally gave up, the Afghan government fell, and the Bush Administration turned its attention elsewhere. The most determined rebels used their American arms to impose the medieval Taliban government, which, among other things, provided a sanctuary where Al Qaida could flourish under Osama Bin Laden.

There is no indication that Bush and his people understood the passions, fears, prejudices, pride, and ambitions of the diverse Iraqi population. For all his faults, Saddam Hussein had imposed peace and order on this potential cauldron. The destruction of his regime opened Pandora's box, much as the end of Tito's communist regime in Yugoslavia did. What will rise in its place is far from clear.

The psychology that motivates radical Muslims to fight endlessly and sacrifice themselves for the cause is difficult for Americans to understand. The religious fear of death, the desire for male domination, the bitter pride of people who have been humiliated, the hatred of Israel, the conviction of ultimate victory, all of these and more confront the pragmatic impatience of the West. The majority of Iraqis probably fear these people and yet applaud their defiance of America. In this context, George Bush's "Mission Accomplished" is rapidly becoming "Mission Impossible."

# A LOGICAL CHOICE

*July 7, 2004*

John Kerry got about as much buzz from his selection of a vice-presidential candidate as he could possibly get. The Great Mentioners had a field day, both in the weeks following Kerry's primary wins and in recent weeks as the Democratic convention approached. He kept the secret well and achieved maximum media attention when the word was finally put out. It was good theater, staged early enough that it was not lost in the ballyhoo of the convention. And for all this drama, Kerry ended up making the logical choice.

I was actually in the Wesley Clark camp, on the assumption that Iraq and the War on Terror would top the issues on voters' minds, but I'll agree with Kerry that Edwards is a better choice. For the first time since Lyndon Johnson helped hold the South for John Kennedy, a vice-presidential candidate may actually influence the outcome of the big race.

The conventional wisdom is that he will not make any difference. The pundits point to Dan Quayle, generally considered an embarrassment to the elder Bush's campaign, who nonetheless did not keep Bush from beating Michael Dukakis in 1988. In the end, so the story goes, voters will decide between the top two men in the context of the economic situation. The vice-presidential candidate on the losing ticket will be forgotten. The one on the winning ticket could end up as president.

When we reflect on that last eventuality, a lot of running-mate decisions have been made for the wrong reasons. Harry Truman was almost an afterthought for Franklin Roosevelt, who was dissatisfied with Vice-President Henry Wallace. Spiro Agnew and numerous others have been chosen for their ability to deliver their home states. Quayle and Jack Kemp were taken to pacify the extreme conservative wing of the Republican Party, while Joe Lieberman was a gesture to the lukewarm Democrats of the DLC. Who remembers William Miller? He was on the Republican ticket in 1964 because no prominent Republican was willing to go down with the Goldwater ship.

The Bush campaign lost no time attacking Edwards as too inexperienced to be president. This is nonsense, of course. Of the men who have become president since World War II, Eisenhower, Carter, Reagan, Clinton, and Bush the younger had no national legislative or governmental experience. Edwards has been in the Senate five years, including service on the Senate Intelligence Committee. In any case, lack of Washington experience has never been a concern of voters. They rightly look at the qualities of the candidate, both tangible and intangible, for clues to future performance.

What, then, is the wisdom in Kerry's choice of a running mate? Is it just the possibility of picking up Edwards' home state of North Carolina, or tipping the balance in Florida? Both of those are possible results, but the choice is a good one for other more important reasons. For someone who has been running neck-and-neck with the incumbent president, John Kerry seems sometimes like the forgotten man of the 2004 election. Try as he does, he has difficulty being heard above the din surrounding George Bush's foray into Iraq. Poll after poll shows people with strong views about Bush, vague ones about Kerry.

Given Bush's problems, this personal dynamic has probably worked in Kerry's favor so far. As the moment of choice nears, however, the choice for voters has to become more clear. Ultimately, voters will have to feel comfortable with Kerry, and his first major decision should be reassuring. Edwards enjoys widespread approval among the voting public, so the choice alone helps Kerry's standing. Edwards is also good at extolling Kerry's virtues. Coming from him, those virtues sound more convincing and less self-serving.

All of this will help Kerry break through as a candidate, but to the extent that the election comes down to a personality contest, Bush will remain a formidable opponent. It is critically important to Kerry's success and the Democratic Party's prospects that a clear Democratic message reach voters this fall. To borrow Emil de Becque's line from South Pacific, "I know what you are fighting against. What are you fighting for?"

The answer is that under Democratic leadership, the national debt will not be allowed to spiral out of control and jeopardize our national standard of living. The tax cuts given recklessly to wealthy Americans will be rescinded and the money put back in circulation to stimulate economic growth. The minimum wage will be raised to an honorable level and the resulting consumer demand will create more jobs, not less. Environmental policy will be based on science, not bought by corporate largess. Energy policy will be based on science, not the whims of oil companies. Medical research policy will be based on science, not the fears of radical religious groups. America's security and reputation in the world will be restored with a renewed commitment to our alliances and the United Nations.

John Edwards can articulate this message wherever he goes, and his personal attractiveness will get him an audience. His magnetism is what he brings to the campaign, and it could make a considerable difference. If Kerry had any reservations about being upstaged, he swallowed them for the sake of a stronger message. There is a word of caution, however.

During the primary campaigns, Edwards tried to make his mark by focusing attention on the poor. He talked about a moral obligation to help the poor and hungry. This was admirable, and it would be an excellent thing to have an advocate of the poor in the vice-presidency. America has paid an enormous social price for its lack of a rational income-support program. When Edwards talked about two Americas, however, it was not clear where much of the middle class fit.

The politics of poverty swung away from Democrats in the 1970s and 1980s. Ronald Reagan exploited it in his rise to the White House. He loved saying, "We declared war on poverty and poverty won." Even such an astute liberal as Bill Clinton felt the need to run away from Democratic compassion and accept a Republican-inspired welfare reform in 1996. It was an unnecessary and unwise reform, but it reflected a political need for Democrats to focus on the working poor and the middle class. This will have to be the case in 2004 as well. The poor economy under Bush has aggravated poverty as well as middle class insecurity. Bringing back a strong job market will do the most for the working poor, while also relieving the fiscal pressure on social programs. This is the message Kerry, and Edwards, must fashion. Edwards has a willing audience awaiting him. He must not miss his chance.

# SPECTATORS

*July 13, 2004*

No matter how much money is spent on the election this year, no matter how much ink is spilled, no matter how much idle chatter fills the airwaves, no matter how much time we spend following and talking about the campaign, the fact is that most of us are just spectators on the sidelines. With a few exceptions, the votes we cast on November 2 will be as meaningless as straws in the wind. The real election will be happening somewhere else.

It is no secret that the presidential campaign is being waged in 17 states, those that could conceivably change sides from their 2000 result. With Kerry's choice of John Edwards, North Carolina has become an 18th player, at least for now. Some analyses have reduced the true battlegrounds to seven or eight. The rest of us will see little of the candidates or their advertising, only their appeals for money. Maybe we should count our blessings.

The culprit in this state of affairs is the Electoral College, that peculiar invention the founding fathers wrote into the constitution. It is not a college, of course, and since at least 1860, it has been only a formality to record the state-by-state results of presidential voting. The practice of awarding all of a state's electoral votes to one candidate has conditioned campaign strategy throughout much of our history. It has magnified the influence of voters in swing states and relegated the rest of us to the role of poor cousins.

Whenever the faults of the system are evident, as they were in 2000, most of us shrug our shoulders, knowing that amending the constitution requires approval by 37 of the 50 state legislatures. Few of us realize that there actually is an alternative. States do not have to award all their votes to one candidate. In fact, Maine and Nebraska award electoral votes by congressional district. If a significant number of states opted for this system, presidential elections would become more broadly competitive.

Or would they? If targeting shifted from the state level to the congressional district level, would more of us be enfranchised? Sadly, the answer is no. Congressional districts are redrawn every ten years to accommodate changes in population. When one party controls the process, the districts are drawn to maximize that party's advantage and protect its incumbents. When the state legislature is divided and a compromise is required, protecting incumbents is the overriding concern. Over the decades, the process has minimized the number of congressional districts where a competitive election may actually occur.

In 2002, Republicans won 52.4 percent of the popular vote for Congress, and emerged with a comparable majority in the House of Representatives. Only 45 of the 435 contests were competitive, however, defined as elections in which the winner got less than 55 percent of the votes. The other 390 were safe in anything short of a political earthquake. In most, the winning percentage was well above 60. The vast majority of these winners were incumbents, of course. In 19 states, all of the incumbents ran for reelection and all won.

In effect, then, at least nine out of ten Americans who vote in the congressional races this year will have no chance of influencing the outcome. This is a more depressing prospect than the disfranchisement produced by the Electoral College. There remains the U.S. Senate, if one happens to live in a state having a Senate election this year. Only 34 of the 100 senators are up for reelection at all. When those 34 seats were last contested in 1998, only 9 met the test of competitiveness, and most of those were in the states considered key to the presidential election. So much for the rest of us. Did the Iraqi people know what they were missing?

If it seems like members of Congress are living in their own world, it's because they are. When an incumbent eventually retires, a spirited contest may ensue in his party's primary. Primaries are low-turnout elections in which voters with extreme views often wield significant power. The Republican Party, in particular, has virtually lost its moderate representatives through the process. The U.S. Capitol now reverberates with diatribes about issues that are all but irrelevant for most of us, while the real power is quietly wielded by lobbyists in designer suits. (State capitols are microcosms of the big show.)

This sorry situation will last as long as competition is kept out of the electoral process. Unfortunately, that could be a very long time. We could wish for another progressive movement, like the one that forced direct election of senators and other reforms in the early 20th century. Alternatively, the courts could intervene. The U.S. Supreme Court has already interpreted the Voting Rights Act to sanction districts favorable to black representation. Perhaps a lawsuit could make its way through the system to require competitive election districts. Perhaps it could begin with one of the states that allow citizen initiatives on the ballot.

One person, one vote, that is the theoretical principle of American democracy. It is honored more in the breach than in practice, however. Without competition, we will never have a responsive political system. We will remain bogged down in back-door deals and mindless rhetoric while our real problems are left to fester.

# THE YEAR OF LYING DANGEROUSLY

*July 14, 2004*

I saw an interesting little piece on television the other day - about lying. It seems someone did an experiment with three-year olds and found that they will instinctively lie if they have broken a rule. They understand that telling the truth may have unpleasant consequences, so they deny it. This is apparently one of those childhood lessons that we carry throughout our lives. The narrator pointed out that most people lie at least once a day.

Of course, most of these are little white lies. We tell them to avoid the unpleasantness of criticizing or disagreeing with someone. We tell them to keep our marriages on an even keel. We tell them to bolster our children's morale and confidence. Life could be hell if we did not lie a little. Look what happened to poor Jim Carrey.

Sometimes the reason for lying is more serious. Bill Clinton clearly wanted to hold on to his wife and family, to avoid hurting them or losing their respect, and lying had worked until the Monica thing got out of the box. Most of us would be tempted to lie in that situation, although some of us might think better of it before we got in too deep. Clinton could have saved himself a lot of trouble if he had owned up and said, "Yeah, I made a big mistake. I hope it doesn't cost me my family."

It is not surprising, then, that George Bush tells a few lies. Having grown up a privileged ne'er-do-well, he had plenty of opportunity to practice. He also seems to have learned something from his initial lie about his Alabama National Guard service. He has actually become a very accomplished liar, who seems to instinctively understand the difference between misleading and outright lying. He is much better than Vice-President Cheney.

When the 9/11 Commission concluded that there was no cooperative relationship between Saddam Hussein and Al Qaeda, Cheney tried to argue with them, implying that he had information linking Saddam to the hijackers. Bush also insisted there had been a relationship, but he emphasized that he had never claimed Saddam was involved in the 9/11 attacks. Technically, this was probably true. However, Bush had lumped Saddam in enough sentences with references to Osama bin Laden and the war on terrorism that a large majority of the American people believed Saddam was involved.

The Senate Intelligence Committee has just released a report that is scathingly critical of the CIA and the intelligence assessment done on Iraq's weapons program before the war. The majority report absolves the Bush Administration of charges that it pressured the CIA to support its desire to invade Iraq. Technically, this may be true. But we know that war with Iraq was a Bush priority from his first day in office, and we know that he ranted about Saddam in the aftermath of the 9/11 attacks. We also know that the Secretary of Defense and the Vice-President were running their own little intelligence shop in competition with the CIA.

In such an atmosphere, the march to war appears inevitable, and must have appeared so to CIA Director George Tenet. Given the weakness of the intelligence data, it is not surprising that the case for war received the benefit of the doubt. Now that the majority of the public has concluded the invasion was a mistake, George Bush would have us believe that he made the only decision he could, based on the information available. This borders on an outright lie. There is no indication that Bush seriously questioned any of the rationales for war, only the way they would "play" with the American people.

A decision to go to war is the most grave that a national leader must make. People will die and be crippled as a result, our soldiers, enemy soldiers, civilians, children. The course of a war can never be known in advance. Once unleashed, it will assume a life of its own, with consequences that cannot be foreseen. Never has this been more evident than in the debacle that has followed our March 2003 invasion of Iraq. We took an unhappy country and made it miserable. We exchanged enormous international goodwill for enormous hostility. We went from being the most respected country in the world to being the most feared.

George Bush has lost credibility with much of the American public, and rightly so. He misleads with such facility that he almost seems to relish it. Without batting an eyelash, he assured us in 2001 that average American families would get tax cuts of $1100, when most would get $300 or less. The "average" he spoke of was heavily weighted by the thousands, even millions, going to the wealthy few. Bush has changed his position on numerous issues in the face of political pressure, but has never acknowledged the reversals. His campaign ads are full of distortions about John Kerry, as his father's were about Bob Dole, and we are told that he personally works on each one.

Deliberately misleading the public about domestic issues is unsavory, although not uncommon. Fabricating a pretense for war, on the other hand, is a frightening practice. Hitler used it in the 1930s to build his central European empire. The U.S. did so in 1845 and 1898 in building our own empire. Lyndon Johnson used the dubious Gulf of Tonkin incident to justify the bombing of North Vietnam. The fact that there is ample precedent for Bush's manipulation of public opinion, however, does not make it any more acceptable.

Under Bill Clinton, we got away from treating international relations as just part of the political game. We made great strides toward a more peaceful, rational world. Clinton was warmly received wherever he went, and American prestige was the highest it had been since World War II. Clinton could not resist lying about his personal failings, but he, and America, had great credibility in the world. Sometimes the truth is too important to ignore. Sometimes lies are too dangerous to trivialize.

# JOB FAIR

*July 17, 2004*

Haliburton held a job fair here in Atlanta this weekend.
Haliburton is the giant engineering and oil services company
formerly headed by Vice President Dick Cheney. Through its
subsidiary, KBR, it is the prime recipient of government
contracts to rebuild Iraq. The advertising did not mention
Haliburton or Iraq, only great overseas job opportunities.
They won't fool many people, I thought. Who in his right
mind would sign up to be a target for ruthless terrorists?

The answer is 30,000 people, by Halliburton's latest
count of its employees in Iraq. Hundreds of people attended the sessions in Atlanta, after 250 had shown up in
Savannah recently. To the company's credit, the recruiters
did not pull any punches. They described the dangers, the
long workdays, the miserable conditions. They also dangled
compensation of $80,000 to $300,000, paid vacations, health
and life insurance, and free rides home for those who
changed their minds.

So who is willing to take the risk? The poor kids 18-21
sought out by Army recruiters? Not hardly. The place was
populated by unemployed engineers, computer specialists,
schoolteachers, human resource managers, truck drivers,
construction workers, people in their 30s, 40s, 50s, even 60s.
Many had not had a decent job for three years. Haliburton
says it has 100,000 applications on file, with the states of the
Deep South heavily represented.

Can anyone imagine this scene four years ago? If there were a more dramatic illustration of what has happened to the American economy and the American middle class in recent years, I would like to hear about it. Of course, the majority is still employed, still getting by all right. But everyone knows someone who is struggling, who is trying to replace a good job with menial or free-lance work, who has lost health insurance, whose severance pay and unemployment benefits have run out, whose spouse is working two jobs to keep them afloat, and so on. In this context, the middle class is losing its sense of security. There but for the grace of God go I.

George Bush is touring the country touting his economic recovery, touting statistics showing a million jobs created this year. Democrats battle back with their own statistics: a net loss of almost 2 million jobs since Bush became president. Six months ago, it was 3 million - the losses have been cut. Bush says the unemployment rate is down from last summer, things are getting better. Kerry says it is still 5.6 percent, compared to 4 percent when Bush took office.

Bush accuses Kerry of painting a pessimistic picture of America, causing Kerry to proclaim his optimism at every opportunity. The American people, however, do not need anyone to tell them how the economy is doing. They can see it with their own eyes and hear it with their own ears. They know that good job opportunities are few and far between, that gas prices are stubbornly high, that major airlines are in bankruptcy or teetering on the brink, that property taxes are rising while school systems struggle to cut costs, that small businesses are surviving but not prospering, that health insurance is becoming more costly and elusive, that sons and daughters graduating from college are finding little to do but go back to school.

The commentators on CNBC scour the numbers weekly for some sign that better times are ahead. They bemoan the reluctance of investors to put money on the table. After a relief rally in 2003, the stock market has drifted lower throughout 2004. This is an ominous sign, because the stock market is a usually reliable indicator of what the economy will do for the next six months. The message has been confirmed by consumer confidence surveys and public opinion polls showing the economy is still the leading issue in the campaign. Economic activity is slowing again.

The U.S. economy spent 2001 in recession and business economists have spent the last three years predicting a recovery. Each little blip after a round of tax rebates has spurred some excitement, but soon smoldered out. There has been no Bush recovery - the economy has dropped back and is bumping along at a lower level. If the 2001 recession could be blamed on cyclical forces and Federal Reserve policy, the persisting weak economy has to be laid at the feet of Bush Administration policies.

Bush and the Republican-controlled Congress revived a discredited theory - if wealthy taxpayers could keep more of their money, they would invest it in job-creating businesses and everyone would benefit. Some of their wealth would trickle down to the rest of us. Moreover, the lost tax revenues would soon be made up by the growth of personal and corporate income, so there would be no long-term budget deficits.

That was the theory of Ronald Reagan's entourage, what the elder George Bush once called voodoo economics. The result in the 1980s was a tripling of the national debt, devaluation of the dollar, a severe aggravation of the gap between rich and poor, and a deep recession in 1991 that cost the elder Bush his presidency. The spotty prosperity of the 1980s centered around heavy military spending purchased with the national credit card.

Since 2001, the Federal Reserve has pumped unprecedented amounts of liquidity into the economy with cheap credit, yet the "recovery" remains anemic. Federal spending is running far above revenue, as the promised economic growth again fails to materialize. The dollar has fallen dramatically, yet the country continues to run a huge trade deficit. In short, we are nearing the limit of what simply printing money can accomplish.

Nothing short of a reversal of economic theory can bring prosperity back to the U.S. The vast sums of money cut from the income tax obligations of the wealthy have mostly gone out of circulation. They reside in bank accounts, foreign real estate and sports cars, vacation homes, and club memberships, but scarcely in job-creating businesses. They have not even gone into the stock market or venture capital funds. They have not, in other words, trickled down.

Economic prosperity results when money circulates briskly. Personal income grows with the pace of transactions. If government wants to stimulate the economy, it must stimulate the demand for goods and services. In short, it must spend money on salaries and purchases. The most effective way to get this money is to tax wealthy households that are spending a low proportion of their income. The money gets back into circulation, is spent quickly by low- and middle-income households, creates more demand, and the velocity of circulation accelerates. Lo and behold, businesses make higher profits, investment returns improve, and the wealthy find themselves with more income. You have the Clinton economic miracle of the 1990s.

Prosperity is demand-driven, so whatever increases demand, other than just piling up debt, will stimulate the pace of economic activity. Investment follows demand, it does not lead it. The lower half of the population will put money into circulation faster than the upper half, the lower 80 percent faster than the upper 20 percent. A long-overdue increase in the minimum wage, so bitterly opposed by businessmen, would soon raise their profits. Wealth may not trickle down, but it certainly does bubble up. As I have said before, it is not rocket science.

Can John Kerry and John Edwards make the argument in such straightforward terms? Probably not. The Republican Party has hammered Democrats so hard with the "tax and spend" label that they must couch their economic policies in veiled terms like "fiscal responsibility." It is remarkable that Kerry even talks about rescinding the tax cuts for households earning over $200,000. He could not do it if Bush had not made his favoritism to the rich so obvious.

If I were advising George Bush on campaign strategy, I would tell him to ignore the economy and talk only about terrorism and gay marriage. If he continues to defend his tax policies and paint a rosy scenario, he will convince the American people that he is as out of touch with the country as his father was. Instead of attending another fundraiser, maybe he should have dropped by the Halliburton job fair. He could have gotten a sense of the real labor market.

# ACCEPTANCE SPEECH

*July 25, 2004*

I cannot say I am looking forward to John Kerry's acceptance speech at the Democratic Convention. Along with the
October debates, this is Kerry's primetime chance to get his
message and persona across to the American people. From
the recent snatches I have heard, however, I am not optimistic. After all this campaigning, he has not lost his annoy-
ing habit of running sentences together and pausing in the
wrong place. I get the impression that if he pauses after
making a good point and lets the audience respond, he will
lose his train of thought.

I am also hearing sound bites that sound like meaningless platitudes. There is a lot about American values and
what Americans can accomplish together and how Kerry
and Edwards are optimistic about the future. I start to think
about that 'bridge to the 21st century" that Clinton and
Gore invoked ad nauseum. I do not think this is what the
people are listening for. I think they are listening for alternatives, for how government would be different if Kerry and
the Democrats won. So, with no modesty, here are my contributions to John Kerry's acceptance speech.

John Edwards and I have been travelling this country
for over a year, listening to Americans from all walks of life.
I think we have a pretty good idea of what is on people's
minds and what really matters to them in this election.

Does anyone here think President Bush and his Republican leaders in Congress are busy on things that really matter? (Pause.)

Judging by the Republican agenda in Washington, Americans should be thinking about how to write a definition of marriage into the U. S. Constitution. They should not be thinking about the miserable job market of the past three years. (Pause.)

Judging by the Republican agenda in Washington, Americans should be thinking about letting gun dealers sell assault weapons again. They should not be thinking about the rising crime rates of the past three years. (Pause.)

Judging by the Republican agenda in Washington, Americans should be thinking about how to turn back the clock on women's rights. They should not be thinking about the single mothers who are working for a totally inadequate minimum wage. (Pause.)

Judging by the Republican agenda in Washington, Americans should be thinking about getting senior citizens to use their wonderful new drug discount cards. (Pause) They should not be thinking about the millions of senior citizens who have lost part of their retirement income in the past three years. (Pause.)

Judging by the Republican agenda in Washington, Americans should be thinking about how to make sure schoolchildren say every word in the Pledge of Allegiance. They should not be thinking about the growing class sizes and lost programs in their schools. (Pause.)

Judging by the Republican agenda in Washington, Americans should be thinking about making sure nobody travels to Cuba. They should not be thinking about the economic disaster that continues to plague the airline industry long after 9/11. (Pause.)

Judging by the Republican agenda in Washington,

Americans should be thinking about making sure family planning is not covered by health insurance. They should not be thinking about the forty-six million Americans with no health insurance at all. (Pause.)

Judging by the Republican agenda in Washington, Americans should be thinking about how to define patriotism. They should not be thinking about the soaring national debt and devaluation of the dollar that has weakened the American economy. (Pause.)

Now I ask you again, are President Bush and the Republican leaders in Congress busy with things that matter most in this election? (Pause.)

Or do they just want to distract voters away from the failures of the past three years? (Pause.)

What can Americans expect from a Democratic president and congress?

First of all, they can expect a government that values international cooperation in the fight against terrorism. The day after the election, I will begin calling world leaders with a message that the United States wants to return to the spirit of collective security that prevailed in the 1990s. We will put a top priority on cooperation among intelligence, investigative, and law enforcement agencies around the globe to root out terrorist organizations and disrupt their plans. This is what we should have done instead of foolishly invading Iraq. (Pause.)

Second, they can expect a reversal of the generous tax cuts given to the wealthy and a return to a balanced budget. We will put federal taxes to work stimulating the economy and creating jobs. A healthy job market will be the number one priority of a John Kerry administration. (Pause.)

Third, the American people can expect serious help for schools and a correction of the mistakes that were made in the "No Child Left Behind Act." (Pause.)

Fourth, Americans can expect a determined focus on solving the national health insurance dilemma once and for all. (Pause.)

Fifth, the people can expect that environmental policy, medical policy, and energy policy will be based on the best available science and not on ideology and corporate power. (Pause.)

Sixth, they can expect a renewal of the ban on assault weapons, which has greatly helped the police departments of this country in the fight against crime. (Pause.)

The list could go on, but I will close with one more expectation. A John Kerry administration will level with the American people. (Pause.) I will instruct everyone in my administration to respect the facts and the truth. We will make certain of our facts and act accordingly. I will not mislead the American people in order to get their support and their sacrifices. (Pause.)

My fellow Americans, a great deal is at stake in this election. The prosperity of our country is at stake. Our role as a constructive leader in the world is at stake. Our tradition of caring about each other when we need help is at stake. Our feelings of security in our communities are at stake. Do not let anyone turn you away from the things that matter most to you. Political leadership is only as good as you require it to be. Hold me to a high standard. Hold us all to a high standard.

I thank you for this historic opportunity.

# ON MESSAGE

*July 30, 2004*

If the discipline of the Democratic Convention is any indication, John Kerry is indeed a strong leader. Will Rogers
used to say that he did not belong to any organized party -
he was a Democrat. Raucous conventions have been a tradition in the Democratic Party, or at least they were until Bill
Clinton came along. Now they are productions, and the dele-
gates are little more than extras to impress the television
audience. Those who got a chance to say something to the
frustrated news reporters stayed cheerfully on message. They
were well prepared.

The convention themes bore the unmistakable stamp of
the two principals. Leadership under fire and restored international prestige was the message from John Kerry. John
Edwards brought the insistence on positive campaigning,
unifying the country, and reveling in the promise of
America. George Bush was hardly mentioned by name,
although his policies and missteps were invoked for listeners
who follow the news enough to catch all the references.

The white-glove approach was a calculation, of course.
The opening blast of Bush-Cheney advertising had been a
shameless distortion of Kerry's record, but millions of dollars had produced no lasting result. Assuming a resumption
of these tactics, Kerry hoped to create a contrast that would
work to his advantage. As for Edwards, he became a poster
boy for positive campaigning in the early primaries and is

convinced it is the way to go.

In earlier columns, I have cautioned against the temptation to personalize the contest with President Bush, both because of public respect for the office and because Bush is good at establishing a simple, down-to-earth rapport with many people. In trying to avoid personal attacks, however, Democrats must not let their rhetoric become so generalized that voters cannot identify the differences between the parties. George Bush and the House Republicans have led an unrelenting assault on every Democratic achievement of the past 70 years. It is important that voters be made aware of this in a clear message.

I did not hear all the speeches, but I only noted two that compared policies using the words "Democratic" and "Republican." One of these was Bill Clinton's opening night salvo, and it was the first time I can remember hearing Clinton use the party labels. I thought he made some inroads on the task of articulating party differences. I found myself wishing (1) that they had given him more time to speak, and (2) that he had made speeches like that during the 1996 campaign.

Nancy Pelosi, the Democratic Leader in the House, made a similar, if less charismatic, effort to articulate party differences. Maybe more than anyone else at the convention, she was aware of the need to broaden public attention beyond the presidential horse race. Democrats have an outside chance to regain control of both houses of Congress, which they will need if they want to roll back the tax policies of the Bush Administration. It will not happen unless a coherent Democratic alternative is offered and voters are asked to vote for the party as well as its presidential candidate.

The standard Democratic approach has been to identify key races and then provide financial and technical assistance to the candidates. Those candidates, in turn, are expected to run strong personal campaigns with emphasis on local issues. For over twenty years now, this has been a recipe for failure. Never was it more evident than in 1994, when Newt Gingrich used the "Contract with America" to nationalize the congressional elections. George Bush repeated the strategy in 2002, leaving Democrats to wonder what had happened on the way to their majority.

Democrats could pull some surprises this year, given the problems of the Bush Administration and the unified energy of the Democratic Party. In Georgia, for example, they could recapture two House seats and hold the Senate seat being vacated by turncoat Zell Miller. To do so, they must reverse the partisan tide that swept the state in 2002, and this can only happen as part of a national tide fueled by a national message. The individual candidates, bless their hearts, will be at the mercy of the larger picture.

What are the components of this message? Let me first say that all the rhetoric about unifying the American people is a waste of time. There is no great divide among the vast majority of us. I play tennis with a group of older people whose political views run the spectrum. We get along just fine. Each day, Americans of different race, nationality, religion, and sexual orientation interact calmly and cheerfully in the business and professional worlds. They share the trains, airport security lines, and highways with courtesy and composure. Americans know how to compartmentalize their political views and preserve a civil order.

What they do want, however, is intelligent public policy that improves their quality of life instead of undermining it. Democrats must convince a majority of voters that they can provide such policy. It begins with restoring balance to the federal budget by raising as much revenue as is needed to fund the services that people want. There is no need to fret about the long-term viability of Social Security and Medicare unless we continue to borrow from those trust funds to cover the shortfalls in general revenue. The government owes these funds a lot of money, and when their surpluses turn to transitional deficits, general revenues will have to repay the debt. We cannot do this if we pile up debt mindlessly year after year.

Under the Clinton Administration, we had a fair and adequate tax structure that both stimulated consumer demand and began to pay down our national debt. We had the luxury of correcting some of the anomalies in the system while preserving its overall effectiveness. Returning to that basic structure would again generate economic growth at a pace to reduce the unemployment rate. Combined with a long-overdue increase in the minimum wage, the accelerated circulation of money would enhance both economic and social well being.

Many things fall into place in a prosperous economy with a robust labor market. When people have opportunities and reason to hope for better times, when they feel they have a stake in a civil society, a number of social ills decline. Property crime, domestic violence, child abuse, and teenage pregnancy all went down substantially under the Clinton Administration. Our sense of personal security was high. All this has changed under the Bush Administration. We may not need speeches about unification, but we do need to bring everybody under the tent. This is a message that people can relate to.

There are other, more specific issues that should be addressed as well, but the basic economic difference is the one that is critical. Democrats should not underestimate the capacity of the voters to understand. Intuitively, a majority already senses that the Democratic Party does a better job managing the economy. All they need is for the party to fill in a few blanks.

# HURRY UP, JOHN

*August 02, 2004*

There may have been a time in his younger years when John Kerry was ahead of public opinion. Maybe he went out on a limb a few times during his Senate career. Since he became a candidate for president, however, he has been consistently trying to catch up. A painful example of this occurred a few days after the Democratic convention.

Wolf Blitzer of CNN was interviewing Kerry and Edwards and asked the following perfectly logical question: "Senator Kerry, you asked in 1971 how does the government ask the last man to die for a mistake. Knowing all we know now, do you think the invasion of Iraq was a mistake?" Ninety percent of Democrats and at least sixty percent of the American public would have unequivocally said yes. Kerry, weighing his words as he pushed them out, gave an answer that was so convoluted I cannot even remember it. Edwards tried to help, but sensing the struggle playing out in his patron's mind, he too lapsed into incoherence.

If questions like this are asked in the October debates (and they will be), George Bush will give simple, forceful answers in defense of all the foolish things he has done. He will get away with it if Kerry persists in hedging every sensible answer with three or four predicates.

In the same interview, Kerry said he would bring a large portion of U.S. troops home from Iraq in his first term.

Excuse me? Nearly a majority of Americans want them out now, and by the time Kerry becomes president, it will probably be a majority. We can attribute this to war weariness, anger at being lied to, or simple logic. If the invasion was a mistake, the occupation is a mistake. This is the logic of public opinion.

Of course, the public can be manipulated, it can be impatient, and it is not necessarily well informed, right? Of course, but I am beginning to wonder if the public understands the Iraq mess better than the politicians. Actually, I think the Bush Administration is looking hard for a way out, having seen the sands of public opinion fall away under their feet. They were hoping the transfer of sovereignty (or whatever it is) to a government arranged by the United Nations would get Iraq off the front pages. It did not work, and I would not be at all surprised if Bush began troop withdrawals before the election. If he lied about the threat, why not just lie about current progress?

It has been an axiom of most national politicians, including Democrats, that, having committed ourselves and destabilized Iraq, we must see it through to the end. We cannot let Iraqi democracy fail, and we cannot let the country become a haven for terrorists. Some very serious and well-informed analysts are beginning to question this consensus, however. The key consideration for the future may be whether the presence of American troops in Iraq is the principal cause of instability and violence. If it is, then the sooner we get them out, the better the chance that the Iraqi people will find some solution that they and the rest of the world can live with.

American forces have been a magnet for Al Qaeda and its fellow travelers to slip into Iraq and practice terrorism against Americans. We are nearing 1,000 dead and 3,000 wounded in Iraq, which means that the human tragedy is approaching 9/11 itself. These foreign terrorists have incited violence and disorder to frustrate America's plans, but they are hardly alone. A majority of the Iraqi people bear a deep and complex resentment toward their occupiers, and violent opposition has become a badge of honor in some sectors of the population.

It is becoming increasingly clear that insurrection against the Americans and anyone who collaborates with us can be the basis of a drive for power as the occupation ends. The longer the Americans stay, the more organized, disciplined, and legitimate this movement can become. If this sounds familiar, then you are old enough to remember the Viet Cong. Iraq had a docile population when we invaded it, but the situation has evolved to one where violent defiance is not only condoned but valued. Iraqis are not yet comparable to the Palestinians, but they are moving in that direction. By staying in Iraq, we may be undermining the moderate elements of the population who want to avoid a bloodbath.

John Kerry cannot discuss this during the campaign, but I hope he is thinking about it. If he is asked the same questions again, I hope he is ready with some straightforward answers. "Yes, the invasion was a mistake because it distracted us from Afghanistan, where the Al Qaeda threat was launched. It cost us the goodwill of our friends and allies around the world, whose cooperation we needed to effectively root out terrorist cells. It destabilized a country that had not been associated with terrorism and made it a dangerous mecca for terrorists. Like everyone else, I listened to all the exaggerations about the supposed threat from Saddam Hussein. I trusted the president to abide by the spirit of the congressional resolution and build a broad coalition through the United Nations. I'm sorry I trusted him."

"How will I deal with Iraq? The day after the election, I will begin calling world leaders, including the leaders of Arab nations, to seek a consensus on how a peaceful and stable Iraq can best be achieved. When that consensus is reached, the role of American aid and American troops will be adjusted to become part of an international solution. We will not keep troops in Iraq any longer than they are absolutely needed and wanted by the Iraqi people."

The American people are tired of hearing doubletalk about Iraq. Kerry and Edwards can afford to be more candid than they have been. They too were misled when Bush insisted on a war powers resolution just before the 2002 congressional elections. There is no shame in regretting a mistake. To err is human, to persist is diabolical.

# CRYING WOLF

*August 11, 2004*

Sometimes I wonder if I'm an alien from another planet, or
maybe I just don't get it. If I were in charge of protecting
the U.S. from terrorism and I had what seemed to be reliable
evidence that an attack was imminent, that narrowed the targets to eight or ten and the means of attack to two or three,
would I be broadcasting this to the world? Or would I be
working covertly to identify the perpetrators and frustrate
their plans?

What purpose was served by Tom Ridge's grave pronouncements last week and the mobilization of police in
New York and Washington, with attendant disruption of
normal activity? If I were a terrorist with a truck bomb
ready in New York, I could drive off to any of several hundred lucrative targets not named by Ridge. In any case, the
"intelligence" on which the whole thing was based turned
out to be anywhere from eight months to four years old.
What made Ridge think an attack was imminent?

Al Qaeda now knows what we know and how we came
to know it. In fact, in its haste to demonstrate its vigilance,
the Bush Administration apparently ruined an undercover
operation in Pakistan that promised some real progress
against the terrorist network. I can never decide if the people running our government are just clowns or really sinister
politicians. Are they deliberately trying to keep Americans
roiled up about terrorist threats to distract them from the

issues of jobs, health care, and education? If so, I don't think it's working. You can cry wolf just so many times.

What the alerts did demonstrate once again was the absurdity of terrorism politics in the U.S. The day after 9/11, I wrote to the few friends who understand my twisted thinking and predicted that Bush would lead the country in a wholly illogical and counterproductive response to the tragedy. Within a few hours, two things were obvious to my mind. First, the attacks were carefully planned, patiently prepared, and synchronized so that preventive measures could not be mounted in time. Once they were over, nothing else was coming in the foreseeable future. Second, the destruction and loss of life were a means to an end - the disruption of the U.S. economy and our open society.

I do not believe we could have prevented the 9/11 attacks, but we could have foiled the larger purpose. Our defiance could have taken a different form, a national commitment to resume business as usual even as we mourned our loss. We could have issued an order to keep cockpit doors locked and end the standard operating procedure of cooperating with hijackers. That would have allowed us to get stranded planes back in the air and airports open for efficient operation. We could have appealed to everyone to hold their events on schedule and dedicate them to our fallen comrades. In short, we could have sent a message to the terrorists that they would not succeed.

We did the opposite. We turned air travel into a nightmare and virtually crushed a major sector of our economy. Washington National Airport was closed for nearly a year. We suspended a whole host of activities for up to two weeks, with enormous collateral damage to the economy. We spent untold billions on extra security at facilities and events with no sense of priority. We kept Americans from visiting the White House and the Statue of Liberty. Congress enacted a major infringement on civil liberties without even reading it, and authorized military action without seriously questioning the logic of it.

The Bush Administration fanned the fires of this national capitulation to terrorism, hurting the economy at least as much as its irresponsible tax policies have done. It would be tempting to call this a colossal failure of leadership, except that it was probably deliberate. The 9/11 attacks were fortuitous for Bush, coming when his approval numbers were falling under the weight of a recession. It surely did not take long for Karl Rove to recognize the political advantage of keeping the nation on a war footing, nor did it take Dick Cheney long to sense the opportunity to settle scores with Saddam Hussein.

The media, of course, served as willing handmaidens to the administration. The media thrives on fear, on "warning" the public of a wide assortment of potential disasters, nearly all of which are wildly exaggerated. By its standards, there is nothing newsworthy in telling people that the probability of any of these things happening to them is negligible. Probabilities are not news. Given the media's readiness to pounce, no local official, no facility manager, and no airport director is going to stand up and say, "Wait a minute, this is silly."

Unfortunately, the Democrats have not shown any more common sense. At least the Republicans have a motive; the Democrats have only timidity. They first reacted to 9/11 by trying to show their solidarity with the president, a gesture that surely must have amused Rove and Cheney. Their docility was reinforced when an anthrax-laden letter showed up in the office of Senate Democratic Leader Tom Daschle, setting off an unprecedented disruption of Senate operations. As good Boy Scouts, they trusted Bush not to politicize the war on terror, and walked quietly into the trap he set for them in the two months before the 2002 congressional elections.

Stung by that defeat, Democrats decided they had to have anti-terrorism policies of their own. They would spend more and fight terrorism with more vigor than the Bush Administration, which was playing its cards in Iraq. Do any older readers hear history repeating itself? Does anyone remember how the Democrats, smarting from the "loss" of China and beaten up by Joe McCarthy, pledged in 1960 to fight Communism more aggressively than Eisenhower had? That rhetoric led us inexorably into the morass of Vietnam.

Today, Democrats are trying to outbid the Bush Administration on homeland security. They are talking about inspecting containers in ports and beefing up border checkpoints. They are talking about the vulnerability of nuclear and chemical plants. They are talking about spending more on "first responders." The possibilities are endless. Let's talk about one of them.

The Port of Los Angeles off-loads two million containers a year. Most are put directly on a chassis for delivery either to a customer or to a waiting stack train a few miles away. Some of them are enroute to Europe, crossing the U.S. by rail. Others are bound for the central and eastern U.S. The railroads and steamship lines have worked hard to hone this process to tight schedules, often to replenish just-in-time inventories. To date, no incidents of potential terrorism have been associated with container traffic, yet we are talking about inserting an inspection procedure into the system. Is that Osama bin Laden laughing that I am hearing?

Americans have been served badly by both parties since 9/11. We should have invested our resources in covert antiterrorist action and demonstrated our national will to conduct our business openly and efficiently. We should not have given the terrorists the satisfaction of knowing that they can disrupt our lives anytime they choose, without even launching a real attack. Would Bill Clinton have sensed this and taken us in a different direction? Maybe not, he has certainly never said so. He was the brightest president we have had. If not him, then who?

# SOAKING THE MIDDLE CLASS

*August 15, 2004*

The Congressional Budget Office is not part of the Bush Administration, although its budget is controlled by the Republican Congress and its director was Bush's first chief economist. Despite these political realities, the CBO, like its sister agency the GAO, is expected to sort the wheat from the chaff and report objectively. Consequently, its projections of the cost of programs and future deficits is often more realistic than those of sitting administrations.

Some time ago, several key Democratic leaders asked the CBO to report on which sectors of the public have benefited most from the Bush tax cuts. The result, while no surprise, puts a stamp of authority on the charge that Bush's tax-cutting agenda has shifted part of the burden away from the wealthy and onto the middle class. Using all federal taxes (but no state and local taxes), the CBO calculated that the top one percent of taxpayers saw their share drop from 22.2 percent to 20.1 percent in 3 years. Households earning $50,000 to $75,000 increased their share from 18.7 to 19.5 percent. The average tax cut for the middle 20 percent of households has been $1,090. For the top one percent, it has been $78,460.

Bush is correct when he says all taxpayers have received some relief from federal taxes. He does not add that more than half of that relief went to the wealthiest ten percent. And contrary to what Republicans would have us think, the federal income tax accounts for a relatively small portion of total taxes. State and local taxes have a regressive impact, taking a higher percentage of household income the less a household earns. When all taxes are considered, the wealthiest one percent of households now pay 33 percent of their income, while the rest of the public averages 30 percent. That is hardly soaking the rich.

Moreover, the overall tax burden on Americans is small compared to other developed countries. Of the 30 nations in the Organization for Economic Cooperation and Development, only South Korea has a lower tax burden than the U.S. In the meantime, federal spending has soared to cover the costs of war and the military buildup, leading the government to borrow at the unprecedented rate of $40 billion per month. The leading purchasers of this debt have been the Japanese, followed probably by the Saudis. Much of the money is borrowed from the Social Security Trust Fund. At this rate, it is not inconceivable that in 20 years, most of our federal taxes will go to pay Social Security and Medicare benefits and foreign creditors.

The use of borrowed money for a binge of military spending was tried during the Reagan Administration, and it produced modest economic growth until coming up against its natural limits. New England, the West Coast, and the South benefited while the vast midsection of the country struggled. A devaluation of the dollar led to a fire sale of American assets, a path we are tracing again today. Eventually, recession in the Rust Belt pulled the whole economy down.

Our economy is teetering again, three years into an anemic recovery from the 2001 recession. The stock market has been forecasting a slowdown since February, and the labor market has weakened for the past three months. A handful of CEOs, including Warren Buffet, have come forward to say the unthinkable - the Republican agenda has been bad for business. Part of the problem has been the impact of that agenda on state and local governments.

For better or worse, state and local governments have come to depend on federal funds for part of their budgetary needs. In the past four years, they have felt the double blows of a weak economy and federal spending cuts that have left them scrambling to cover deficits. A few state governments have managed to increase sales taxes, but most have passed the problem down to the local level. There, property reassessments and fee increases have wiped out the federal tax relief for the middle class. School districts have increased class sizes, raised health insurance costs for employees, and held raises to a bare minimum. The economic stimulus that state and local spending provides has shrunk, even as local taxpayers are asked to pay more.

Our economy depends on consumer spending, and the income of low- and middle-level families is recycled much faster than that of wealthy families. Government spending on salaries, contracts, and benefits is a key component of that income. When it is reallocated to tax cuts for wealthy families and interest payments to foreign creditors, one of the engines of economic growth is stunted. The federal income tax is the most progressive tax we have in this country, and hence is the most effective at stimulating consumer spending. It assures that some of the excess income flowing to CEOs will get back into the economy. As in the Clinton Administration, that will translate into higher corporate profits, higher bonuses, and higher investment returns.

I do not know whether President Bush was aware of the CBO report when he let slip the other day that he would like to consider a national sales tax as an alternative to the income tax. Is this his agenda for a second term? A national sales tax would shift the burden even more radically onto the middle class. Between the CBO report and the president's comment, Democrats have a golden opportunity to put the tax issue into proper perspective for the voters. Can they overcome their fear of the issue long enough to use it to their own advantage?

# SCHOOL DAZE

*August 21, 2004*

Schools have been in the news lately, as they often are. The test scores were publicized over the summer, revealing that Georgia third-graders were not living up to expectations. They were doing a little better, yes, but not up to the standards that big brother has set for them. I wonder if these pint-sized kids realized how much was riding on them and how many careers they have jeopardized.

Former Georgia Governor Roy Barnes, who bragged during the 2002 campaign that his school reforms were patterned on those of Texas Governor George W. Bush, wrote a blistering column denouncing the failure of Georgia teachers to deliver on his promises. It is doubtful he lost any friends, however, since Barnes was already despised by most of Georgia's teachers.

A study reported in the New York Times found that charter schools, those that have been excused from the rigid control of bureaucracy, were not turning in better test results than their harassed counterparts in the public system. Charter schools exist for a variety of purposes, including meeting the special needs of some students. The study did not, could not, measure whether they were succeeding in their missions, only that their standard test scores were not remarkable.

Finally, a passing article in the Atlanta Journal

Constitution noted that the Georgia Board of Education had agreed to let local districts save money by putting up to 30 pupils in high school science classes, 6 over the state goal established several years ago. Any science teacher trying to cope with 30 students will probably cut to a minimum the amount of hands-on activity and fall back even more on rote preparation for standard tests. Perhaps some of the students can still muster up some enthusiasm for biology, chemistry, and physics.

With the possible exception of poverty, no issue has been the subject of more shameful exploitation by politicians than public education. Sensing a potential constituency among senior citizens, single people, and parents using private schools, conservative Republicans have tapped into the resentment that many of these people harbor toward property taxes. Although parents are generally supportive of their schools and sympathetic toward the teachers, conservative politicians have missed few opportunities to trumpet school failure and belittle the efforts of teachers.

Public schools once enjoyed wide support in both political parties, although the Democratic Party had to manage the hard feelings of its Catholic constituents and the resistance of Southern Democrats to integration. As economic and religious conservatism took control of the Republican Party in the 1980s, the party adopted a position of increasing hostility to public education and a strategy of privatization.

The centerpiece of the strategy has been vouchers, grants of public money that a family could use to pay tuition at any school. Voucher schemes have routinely been quashed by federal courts on the grounds that they violate the constitutional separation of church and state. The Supreme Court is now closely divided on the subject, however, and George Bush's reelection could result in a Court that would change a long-observed principle. The threat to public schools is obvious, and although vouchers could be used by any family, location and transportation realities are likely to limit their use to middle and upper middle class neighborhoods.

In the meantime, schools have become pawns in a cynical political game. All politicians want to be seen as pro-education. The elder George Bush proclaimed himself the "education president," while his son made his supposed Texas educational miracle a centerpiece of his presidential campaign. Republicans found that they could wave the education flag while deploring the poor performance of American schoolchildren and berating teachers, who voted mostly Democratic anyway.

As the Barnes example illustrates, Republicans were not alone in using the schools for political purposes. Moreover, Democrats came to believe that they could not get adequate funding for schools unless they insisted on more accountability. No less a veteran legislator than Ted Kennedy fell into the trap. Desperate to salvage federal aid to education, he negotiated what he thought was a compromise with George Bush. The "No Child Left Behind" Act would require elaborate testing for both school evaluation and student advancement. In return, federal funding would increase and extra resources would be provided to schools most in need.

Bush got exactly what he wanted - the opportunity to cite his "No Child Left Behind" Act at every opportunity but with nothing more than a moral obligation to provide funding. Backed by a Republican Congress and confronted with budget deficits of his own making, he conveniently retreated from the moral obligation. Schools went on a diet of rigorous testing but got nothing in return. They were set up for failure.

Several years ago, some school systems had probably gone too far with "innovative" education at the expense of the basics, and many systems had opted to advance students through the grades rather than endure the hassle of holding them back. Discipline was lax at many schools, especially those serving large populations of low-income households. These were valid issues. They should have prompted a national debate over fundamental questions. Instead, the typical political response was to blame someone, and teachers were conveniently there to blame.

The malaise in American education is not new, but it was exacerbated by the incredible diversity in the schools that resulted from integration plans, a wave of immigration, and the requirement to "mainstream" students with an assortment of special needs. At the heart of the malaise is the American tradition that education through high school should be "one size fits all," with only modest deference to the notion that young people are not all alike. The struggle between educational uniformity and student diversity has been the defining fact of life for American schools and school districts for decades. Classroom teachers cope with it everyday.

No other country faces a comparable degree of cultural and economic diversity, yet most countries provide more educational options to match the needs and desires of young people. By most accounts, those educational systems deliver more public satisfaction and generate less controversy than ours. American schools provide options to high-achieving students in the form of advanced-placement courses and a handful of special-purpose schools. Affluent families can seek appropriate options outside the public system. What we lack are quality schools and programs for young people who are not college-bound. Any attempt to move in this direction is immediately labeled anti-democratic or worse. Unable to provide a large proportion of young people what they might enjoy and appreciate, we provide them nothing at all.

In the meantime, schools burdened with disproportionate numbers of bored young people, along with many who are trying hard to learn in a new language, are condemned and penalized for low test scores. Their high-achieving students are encouraged to transfer, their faculty is ridiculed, their resources are cut, their classes get larger, and they can expect lower test scores next time. Should we expect a rush of high-quality teachers and principals to volunteer for these situations?

Schools are a useful political football, and we cannot expect to hear any realistic or constructive debate about them during this election campaign. The conservative Republican agenda is clear - to discredit public education enough to minimize the resources devoted to it, and to find a formula for redirecting those resources to private education. The Democratic agenda is clouded by a desire to protect public education while somehow accommodating public dissatisfaction.

No politician is going to suggest fundamentally rethinking the goals and structure of our educational system. That could only come from the scholars and practitioners of the profession itself. What John Kerry and John Edwards and other Democratic candidates could do is come to the defense of America's beleaguered public school teachers. They could talk about the difficult task those teachers face every day and of the time when we honored their profession and trusted them to know how to teach our children. They could promise to support public schools rather than making them the scapegoat for our social problems.

Perhaps we cannot come to grips with the underlying problems facing public education. As Democrats, however, we can at least change the tone of the debate.

# ROCKING THE BOAT

*August 28, 2004*

For more than two weeks, the media has focused on television ads by a group called Swift Boat Veterans for Truth, disputing John Kerry's version of events in Vietnam that occasioned his medals and purple hearts. Enough independent accounts have surfaced by now to establish that truth is the last thing these veterans are interested in. Still, polls seem to show that Kerry has been hurt by this latest version of the "big lie."

While members of the broadcast media have bemoaned the resort to such tactics, they have nonetheless savored the opportunity to stir up controversy, and in the process have given the ads much more air time than was paid for. Such is the sway of the profit motive in American broadcast journalism.

If the media and unscrupulous wealthy Republicans can be condemned, however, Kerry and his advisors must accept a share of the responsibility for this bumpy ride. Believing they had to overcome George Bush's natural advantage as the reigning commander-in-chief, they made Kerry's Vietnam service the cornerstone of the Democratic convention. Speaker after speaker, including the Clintons, extolled the nominee's decision to serve and his performance as a patrol boat commander, never mentioning that his tour of duty was only four months long. Kerry himself took a cheap shot at Bush by saluting as he took the podium and announcing he was "reporting for duty."

The most critical decision to be made in a presidential campaign is the choice of issues to focus on, those to play down, and those to simply mention. By giving so much airplay to Kerry's role in a nearly forgotten war, his campaign elevated it to the status of a major issue. In the process, they invited the scrutiny of voters to what he did both during and after the war. Kerry had little to gain from this. By the time of the election, nearly all voters would have known that he served in Vietnam, would have respected him for it, and would have made their choices based on their perception of the current state of the Union. Now, fairly or unfairly, his credibility has become an issue.

The irony of this is that Bush had already handed Kerry the winning issues with policies that stalled the economy and embroiled us in foolish quarrel with the rest of the world. The fallout from these policies is producing a steady drumbeat of bad news for the Administration. The budget deficit climbs inexorably. An official study shows the middle class shouldering a higher share of the tax burden. Others document a growing percentage of families living in poverty and a growing number without health insurance. Despite historically low inflation, the real income of American workers is declining.

All Kerry has to do is quote these government studies. He hardly needs a speechwriter. As for Iraq, he really does not have to say anything at all. The war has become one of those issues that provide their own daily headlines. It is one case where the media's preoccupation with bad news is a boon to the challenger. It is eating away at Bush's standing despite Kerry's ineffective efforts to distinguish himself from the president.

When Bush or his spokespeople try to address the economic and social issues, their gyrations are almost pathetic.

They deny responsibility for the first two-and-a-half years of decline and claim the economy has turned a corner thanks to Bush's tax cuts. They admit that things are still slow, but plead for a little more time to show results. They imply that Congress is holding up presidential initiatives, ignoring the fact that Republicans control both houses of Congress and gave Bush virtually all the tax cuts he asked for. They portray trial lawyers as the primary cause of our health care problems.

It is doubtful that the economy has turned a corner. The stock market, the dollar, and consumer confidence are all signaling a slowdown or, at best, stagnation. Oil prices are hanging stubbornly above $40 a barrel, punishing the airlines and dampening the retail business. All the revisions of job and GDP statistics have been downward. The Democrats could hardly ask for more. Kerry and Edwards are doing their best to keep the focus on the economy and the struggles that many Americans are enduring. It is not enough, however, just to talk about those who have lost their jobs or their health insurance. Most voters still have an income and health insurance. Most voters do not live in poverty.

What is not getting across is the broader effect of these conditions on the rest of us. My upper-middle class neighborhood, for example, is experiencing a crime wave for the first time in years. People are being robbed in parking lots, cars are being broken into on the streets, things are being stolen from carports. When people cannot find a legal way to support themselves and their families, they may resort to crime in desperation. We had enormous declines in crime rates during the prosperous 1990s and now we are going the other way.

The weak job market is hurting not just those who have lost jobs, it is dragging down wages and salaries for everyone. The median household income has declined for three straight years after rising throughout the Clinton Administration. Americans are selling themselves for less because opportunities are scarce. The small tax cuts that most of them received are not much consolation. The weakened dollar is felt by every American who travels abroad or buys gasoline made from imported oil. We have not yet felt the sting of high real interest rates, but they will come if the budget deficit is not brought under control.

Our social fabric has weakened under the Bush Administration. Many Americans seem to sense this when they tell pollsters that the country is on the wrong track. This is the story that Democratic candidates should be telling, and they should use it to emphasize the differences between Democrats and Republicans. Instead of shying away from the party labels, they should be using them to lower the personality content of the campaign. The Democrats have a stronger card to play than just Kerry vs. Bush, and who did what 35 years ago.

The best chance for Kerry and for Democrats running in close races around the country is to ride a partisan wave to victory. For some reason, they continue to downplay the contrast of the last three years with the peace, prosperity, and social progress of the Clinton Administration. Moreover, Democrats seem to think that if they use the word Republican, they will hurt somebody's feelings. Republicans have no qualms about characterizing the "Democrat Party." Conservative Republicans, who are far to the right of many Republican voters, have put us in the fix we are in. Democrats have righted the ship of state before, and they should take credit for it. Ask the voters to put the country back on the right track.

# IS BUSH A CONSERVATIVE?

*September 5, 2004*

The conventions are over, and early returns suggest the Republicans got the bigger bounce. They showed once again their superiority at manipulating public opinion, letting Vice President Cheney and turncoat Zell Miller do the dirty work of bitter personal attacks while George Bush delivered his simple homilies and recalled his promise to be a "compassionate conservative."

It was a nauseating exercise in hypocrisy. Where does Dick Cheney get off accusing John Kerry of being unfit to command the armed forces? Kerry commanded forces in combat, while Cheney did everything he could to avoid military service. As for Bush's compassionate conservatism, there is nothing he can point to in his first term that was compassionate, if we understand by that term having an empathy for people who have not had life handed to them on a silver platter.

A more interesting question is whether Bush, Cheney, DeLay, and their crowd have given conservatism a bad rap. Is favoritism to the rich at the expense of everyone else a hallmark of conservatism? Is opposition to personal rights in every area except entrepreneurship a hallmark of conservatism? Is disregard for future generations a hallmark of conservatism? Is profligate borrow-and-spend management a hallmark of conservatism? Is contempt for science a hallmark of conservatism?

How would the great conservative leaders of the past, Washington, Hamilton, Lincoln, T. Roosevelt, and Eisenhower have viewed this spectacle? Would they have condoned the cynicism with which this group sacrifices the public welfare for the sake of power? Would they have approved the use of hate and prejudice and fear to disguise an agenda of narrow selfishness? Did they believe that the natural wealth and beauty of this country should be parceled up among the most avaricious and ambitious among us? Would they have tolerated a budget deficit of a half-trillion dollars?

What is conservatism anyway? If we get back to fundamentals, it should be a belief in conserving that which sustains a desirable way of life. On one level, this should entail a careful and balanced use of natural resources to assure their availability to future generations. The native Americans of the Great Plains lived for centuries in concert with the great Bison herds from which they drew sustenance, always following rules of conservation. Unfortunately, political neglect in the U.S. has often encouraged reckless exploitation without regard to consequences.

Conservatism has been historically associated with social hierarchy. Human societies have nearly always divided into a privileged minority and a less fortunate majority. The survival of privilege has rested partly on force of arms, but even more on strategic alliances. In much of continental Europe, including Russia, the monarchies and nobility relied heavily on the church to maintain control. This worked well for centuries, until revolution swept away the old order beginning in 1789 and culminating in 1918.

In Germany and Great Britain, the aristocracy made room for a middle class, with whom it shared some of the trappings of privilege. Moreover, under the influence of Bismarck and Disraeli, the ruling classes of Germany and

Britain extended a measure of social security to the working multitude, blunting the revolutionary fervor that infected the rest of Europe. The German aristocracy lost control to National Socialism in the Great Depression, but their counterparts in Britain hung on until the demise of the British Empire.

America had no aristocracy, but its affairs were dominated by the prominent colonial families until the Civil War. After that, great fortunes were made from exploiting the continent, and conservatism began to reflect the values of powerful corporations. In the Republican Party, only Theodore Roosevelt and a few progressives like Robert La Follette and George Norris stood against the tide. Roosevelt was hardly a threat to big business, but he tried to curb its excesses to prevent the rise of radicalism. He took a stand against monopolies and child labor, while remaining a foe of unionism.

When the Depression threatened the reign of American capitalism, a conservative of a different nature took command. Franklin Roosevelt, a scion of old money, saw the need to balance the power of capital and aspirations of labor if the free enterprise system were to survive. The "great negotiation" became the foundation for economic and social progress, with the federal government as arbiter of the equilibrium. With avarice no longer in vogue, the economic tent could be greatly enlarged, at least for white Americans.

Bitterness did not disappear from the boardrooms, but neither did the Republican Party wish to remain in the wilderness. They turned to a common-sense conservative, Dwight Eisenhower, to lead them out. Ike insisted that the New Deal battles were over, that the country needed time to rest and recover. Harry Truman's goal of national health insurance was shelved, and Eisenhower was a reluctant player in the looming civil rights drama, but Social Security and labor legislation were honorably administered. The silencing of Joe McCarthy allowed Americans to enjoy a decade of civility.

Strident conservatism returned with the libertarianism of Barry Goldwater and the class conflict of Ronald Reagan. By the end of the first George Bush presidency, the social fabric of the country was again starting to unravel. Unemployment, poverty, crime, and family dysfunction had all risen to alarming levels. Remarkably, it took only a modest redistribution of wealth under Bill Clinton to turn the situation around, setting the table for gradual progress in a new century.

In 2000, a poor campaign and a dubious election administration opened the door to the most narrow-minded brand of Republican government since the 1920s. The current Bush Administration has elevated personal greed and corporate indulgence to the level of constitutional principles. They dismiss broader notions of the public interest with ridicule and contempt. Social discontent is simmering again, and while revolution is not to be feared, incivility is starting to raise its ugly head.

I have long believed that liberals are the true conservatives. Western Europe escaped communism after World War II largely because social democrats led in the creation of mixed economies and welfare states. The New Deal stopped short of a welfare state, but it gave the American working class a stake in the future. I consider myself a liberal, but what I want most is to live in a civil society. I want people to feel safe in their homes, neighborhoods, schools, and places of work. I want to interact with people of different backgrounds and circumstances and not feel that either of us threatens the other.

This can happen only if we all have something to lose

from the breakdown of order. What has characterized much of the third world is a great gulf between rich and poor, between dominant ethnic group and oppressed majority. The result has been a cycle of violence and unrest, rebellion and suppression, deprivation and tragedy. The United States is not in danger of becoming a third world country, but neither are we setting the kind of contrasting example that we could. Under the Bush version of conservatism, we are going in the wrong direction.

# THE BIG FIVE

*September 13, 2004*

Believe it or not, the election is less than eight weeks away. It is hard to remember what life was like before the campaign. The Kerry camp is going through another bout of sagging poll numbers, occasioning another effort to refocus public attention on the issues that really matter. There is not much time left.

The Democratic ticket has not yet lost the election, but they squandered their lead with a classic miscalculation. Facing an opponent with low approval ratings but a decisive style, they assumed that they had to establish Kerry's credentials as a stronger leader. In so doing, they opened the book on his life and career, revealing someone who is more deliberative and introspective than self-assured. The Republicans were more than willing to exploit every contradiction they could find or invent.

Kerry may ultimately hold his own in this battle, especially if he comes across as presidential in the October debates, but a lot of momentum has been lost. The winning strategy for Kerry and the Democrats was to make the election a referendum on George Bush and the failures of his administration. Kerry and Edwards had to appear competent, knowledgeable, and caring, but they did not have to seize the spotlight from Bush. By trying to do so, they have drawn public attention away from the five major issues that Bush's leadership has created. The Republicans could not have hoped for a better turn of events.

The number one issue that the Kerry campaign should have kept constantly in the public mind is the poor performance of the economy - the weak job market, the stagnation of family income, and the loss of savings in the stock market. Bush's current attempt to convince the public that things are getting better does not ring true with many people, and Kerry could invoke public opinion to support his contention that the recovery is anemic. Throughout the summer, his advertising should have included testimonials from average Americans questioning whether Bush is really in touch with life in these United States.

Closely related is the issue of the deficit. Kerry mentions it, of course, but he does not give it the punch that it could have. Polls have consistently shown that Americans are not comfortable with a burgeoning national debt and consider balancing the budget to be a higher priority than tax cuts. The Bush Administration has added more that a trillion dollars to the national debt and much more is on the way. None of Bush's promises have come remotely close to reality and there is no reason why Kerry should not constantly remind people of those promises. Reckless tax cuts have jeopardized not only Social Security and Medicare benefits, but many of the essential services that government would provide to future generations.

Rising health insurance premiums and copayments have been a fact of life in recent years. American companies, plagued by sluggish revenues and intense competition, have looked at health insurance as a prime candidate for cost-cutting. Many families have opted for higher deductibles to save on premiums, which helps only if everyone stays healthy. Retiree health plans are being cut or discontinued. Medicare premiums have increased much faster than retirement benefits. Along with the rising cost of prescription drugs, this has pressured the standard of living of senior citizens. Yet those with health insurance may consider themselves lucky, since it is out of reach for some 46 million Americans. The Bush Administration has done nothing to address the health care problem except for an ill-conceived Medicare prescription drug program.

These three domestic issues should be the bread and butter of the Democratic campaign, the fodder for the most telling sound bites and all of the advertising. At the same time, Democrats should miss no opportunity to remind voters of Bush's two great failures in the war on terrorism. The invasion of Iraq accomplished nothing to deter terrorism, and actually diverted resources from the struggle against terrorist organizations in Afghanistan and elsewhere. Kerry has finally started to talk about "the wrong war in the wrong place," and he should continue this line of offense.

The Bush Administration's arrogant attitude toward the United Nations and our NATO allies has brought hostility toward the United States to an all-time high. Kerry should stop worrying about Bush's slogan that nobody should have a veto over our national security. A forceful case can be made that we need cooperation with countries all over the world if we are going to combat terrorism effectively. Kerry should promise in every speech to restore good working relations with friendly nations and put the emphasis clearly on destroying the terrorist networks.

Getting the campaign refocused on these five major issues rather than personalities can be accomplished more readily if party history is invoked. Republicans presided over the collapse of the U.S economy in 1929 and left the country mired in the Great Depression. Since World War II, eight of the ten recessions have occurred during Republican administrations. Economic growth has been stronger, unemployment has been lower, and household income has increased faster under Democratic presidents. The most impressive prosperity of the twentieth century occurred under the leadership President Clinton. Rather than shunning party comparisons, Kerry and Edwards should be using them to blunt the personal attacks.

The planets are aligned again for a Democratic victory in 2004. The Republicans know this well, and they are leaving no stone unturned in their bid to frustrate the logical outcome. At this juncture, they appear to be succeeding, but there is still time. Hubert Humphrey came back from a large deficit in 1968 and nearly pulled out a win by getting back to basics. The Democratic base is motivated like never before, a factor that may not be fully reflected in the polls. It is still the Democrats' election to win, if they get their act together.

# THE SILENCE OF THE LAMBS

*September 20, 2004*

The polls are bouncing around like the stock market now.
They are providing a lot of fodder for the pundits, all trying
to prove they are smarter than the candidates.
Recriminations are flying from consultants who were left out
of the campaigns. Young operatives are living from poll to
poll, their moods rising and falling. It is curious that people
have so soon forgotten how misleading were the polls leading up to the Democratic primaries. They can be even more
misleading at this stage in the general election.

To understand the polls, one needs to remember that
politics carries a low priority in the minds of many people.
Admittedly, this year is a little different from most election
years. By all indications, the level of public attention is higher and the partisan bases are definitely more motivated. The
basic reality, however, is that when John Q. Voter answers a
call from a polling organization, it may be the first time he
has tried to make up his mind about the candidates. It is
likely that 25-30 percent of respondents fall in this category.
The call forces some of them to make a premature choice,
but they really represent the large pool of uncommitted voters.

About 65 percent of Americans consider themselves
Democrats or Republicans. The rest call themselves inde-
pendents, but probing by the Survey Research Center of the
University of Michigan has revealed that many of these

actually lean to one or the other party. Only about 10 percent are truly unattached, and these people are the least interested, least informed, and least likely to vote. Party identification and leaning once favored the Democrats, reaching a high point in 1964, but has since evolved to near parity. Other things being equal, this should make for very close national elections.

A key judgement that pollsters have to make is whom to count among their respondents. Some results are reported for all registered voters. Now that voter registration has been broadened through the driver license process, predicting who among those registered will actually vote has become even more problematic. Most polls, however, try to make that judgement and report results for "likely voters." Needless to say, the criteria by which this judgement is made will have considerable effect on the outcome. Democrats, for example, have a better turnout record in presidential elections than in off-year elections. Republican do also, but not to the same extent. Unattached voters have an even greater differential. This year has seen a surge in young voter registration, a factor hardly captured at all in the polling.

Unlisted numbers used to be a problem, but pollsters have gotten around that by using random-digit dialing. They still encounter a fair number of call screeners and uncooperative respondents. Little is known about these potential voters, although they are probably not strong partisans.

The upshot is that polls may be able to tell us which states are close and which are one-sided, but their ability to predict the November outcome is even less reliable than their statistical margin of error. They start to become meaningful in the final week, when a substantial number of voters feel obliged to make their decisions, including whether they really care enough to vote. Even at the end, they may miss the story. Democratic leaders went to bed on election eve

2002 believing they would hold the Senate and gain seats in the House. But their lack of a national message had left many of their "leaners" unmotivated, and they were blindsided by a low turnout.

The Kerry campaign, worried about some of the polls, can take comfort from their shortcomings. There is still a bedrock of intense anti-Bush feeling in the land that will be counted on November 2. The recent speed bumps seem to have convinced Kerry to ride this feeling and focus on the Bush failures. Kerry is a good and intelligent man, but he does not inspire enthusiasm, maybe not even comfort. He has nothing to gain from making himself the center of attention. This election is about Bush, about whether Americans are willing to risk their standard of living for another four years. Kerry has seven weeks to remind voters of this choice.

For some reason, Democrats, and their presidential candidates in particular, have an aversion to using their party's accomplishments in making their case against the Republicans. Just about every public benefit that Americans enjoy was enacted by Democrats over the objection of most Republican politicians. All the reforms of the New Deal - Social Security, Fair Labor Standards, Deposit Insurance, a host of public works projects, and others - were put in place by Democrats. Medicare, which has relieved so many senior citizens and their children of worry about crippling medical costs, was part of Lyndon Johnson's legacy. Fuel economy standards, which helped us escape our first energy crisis, were passed by a Democratic congress over the objections of the auto industry and their Republican allies. The same can be said of environmental protection. Democrats are now fighting to save all of these initiatives, which only a few years ago were taken for granted.

These are critical issues for Americans' quality of life,

and there is a wide gulf on them between Democrats and the hard-liners who have taken over the Republican Party. We hear little about this in the campaign, however. Democrats seem to assume that the voting public is well aware of the differences, and that the story of Democratic achievements need not to be articulated every two years, or even every four years. They are missing an important opportunity. Much of the public is too young to know this history, and many others could use reminding.

Too many potential voters lapse into the observation that the parties are pretty much the same. They would like someone to give them a reason for preferring one to the other. Choosing between the candidates strikes many people as choosing the lesser of two evils. Give them a clear choice between the parties, a rational reason to vote Democratic, and they are more willing to tolerate the shortcomings of a candidate.

This election remains largely a referendum on the Bush administration. The president has made melodramatic pronouncements, backed away from them, shifted his ground, and never admitted to any mistakes. His credibility gap alone is enough to vote him out of office. More important, however, is the threat he and his congressional allies pose to the social and economic traditions of this country, to the broader definition of the public welfare that the Democratic Party represents. Make no mistake, they are determined to tear down that legacy. Democrats have seven weeks left to defend it. They need to give their lukewarm followers a reason to vote, and the uncommitted a reason to vote Democratic.

# DEBATE TIME

*September 27, 2004*

Finally, the climactic phase of this marathon campaign is
here. The first presidential debate is looming, and seems
likely to arouse more than the usual interest. The situation is
similar to 1980 and 1992, when voters were dissatisfied with
incumbent presidents - Carter and Bush - but unsure about
the challengers - Reagan and Clinton. In both years, the
debates gave the challengers a platform to show off their
personal skills and win over enough viewers to carry the day.
Both, incidentally, were helped by third party candidates,
John Anderson in 1980 and Ross Perot in 1992.

    Ralph Nader's candidacy is hurting Kerry this year, so
the personal opportunity is even more important. It is also a
significant challenge. Kerry has tried hard to connect with
people, playing up his combat service, appearing in casual
open shirts, and speaking more directly and forcefully, but he
remains a distant figure for many voters. He has not been
able to shake the Republican characterization of him as
indecisive and contradictory. Hence the paradox that many
people who acknowledge the damage that Bush has done to
our economy and international reputation nonetheless trust
him more to lead the war against terrorism.

    Previous opponents have made the mistake of underes-
timating Bush in debates. He might do very poorly at the
Oxford Union, but he understands the dynamics of televised
political debates in the U.S. He knows that many Americans

are lightly informed, which means that if he speaks decisively using familiar phrases, he can get away with any version of events that he pleases. He also knows that most of the voters he is courting do not travel abroad, have little understanding of the complexities of international relations, and respond easily to patriotic slogans. We can expect a healthy dose of them.

John Kerry is intellectually uncomfortable with simplistic assertions. In the primary campaign, he suffered from overly measured responses to the no-nonsense positions of Howard Dean. He prevailed over Dean and other contenders because of his military and foreign policy resume, which he and many Democrats assumed would be enough to overcome a swaggering commander-in-chief. It has not been. So far, Kerry has not been able to gain the upper hand as a potential leader in the struggle against terrorism.

So Kerry enters these debates as the underdog. The conventional wisdom is that George Bush does not have to hit a home run, just a few singles and maybe a double to hold his advantage. Kerry, it is assumed, must score at least a technical knockout.

Maybe not. Since Labor Day, Kerry has taken a harder line on the Bush record. Like it or not, the campaign is now a contest to drive up the negatives of the candidates. That has been the Republican strategy from the beginning, but Kerry and Edwards tried the upbeat approach throughout the summer. They cannot afford it now. The debates will present a golden opportunity to drive up the Bush-Cheney negatives, providing it is done right.

A tried and true strategy in such debates is to needle your opponent into losing his cool. Sometimes an aggressive questioner does this, as when Bernard Shaw embarrassed Michael Dukakis with a jarring question about the death penalty. (Dukakis actually kept his cool too well, when people thought he should have shown more emotion.) The best way to avoid a bad passage is to follow the precept that the best defense is a good offense. Kerry needs to turn every question into a barb aimed at Bush. He should do the same with Bush's barbs at him. Bush himself is good at this, but he has yet to prove that he can take it as well as dish it out. At times, he has reacted testily to criticism, and this should be one of Kerry's goals.

An example of turning criticism away could come when Kerry is asked about the charge that he has wavered in his position on Iraq. Kerry could say, "The president has been going around telling everyone that I've changed my mind about Iraq, but I've been consistent from the beginning about how I would have handled the situation differently. He is the one who has flip-flopped around. He's changed his reason for going to war at least four times. He belittled the United Nations and then begged it to come in and set up an interim government and elections. He thumbed his nose at our allies and then went to them hat in hand for help. He declared the major fighting over and then warned of a long, dangerous struggle. He says things are getting done and then somebody else in his administration contradicts him."

Kerry has to accomplish this strategy without being too combative or abrasive. He should refer to his opponent at "the president" rather than by name. When he is not speaking, his should listen calmly, take a few notes, and resist any temptation to react with facial expressions or utterances. He has to be aware that people will be watching him, that sometimes the camera will switch to him when he is not expecting it. He should be respectful and patient waiting for his turn, then decisive when it is his turn.

The debates are an important opportunity for Kerry, but they are not a "Hail Mary" situation. The election is still close, and Bush is very vulnerable on his credibility. Kerry can exploit this by invoking Republican senators, members of the administration, and people like Richard Clarke who left in frustration. The first debate is about foreign policy, where Bush is ahead. All Kerry has to do is sow doubts about Bush's leadership in the area that is central to the president's campaign. The next debate will give Kerry a much better opportunity to paint Bush as a friend of the rich who has squandered a prosperous economy and budget surplus.

# CASHING IN

*October 5, 2004*

Debate number one went well for the Democrats, maybe better than they expected. John Kerry's performance was not flawless, and he still has awkward moments trying to explain his votes on the Iraq war powers resolution and the supplemental appropriation. However, only committed Republicans seem to have held it against him, as George Bush's fumbling behavior overshadowed Kerry's shortcomings.

Kerry scored some telling points, as when he reminded Bush that Osama bin Laden and Al Qaeda, not Saddam Hussein, had attacked us. He also calmly refuted Bush's praise of certainty by pointing out that one can be certain but wrong. He followed up by accusing Bush of making a "colossal blunder" by invading Iraq instead of pursuing Al Qaeda.

The post-debate polls quickly put Kerry back in the hunt, negating at least temporarily the effect of millions of dollars in misleading advertising by the Bush campaign. He could now go into the debate on domestic issues on an even footing. Moreover, the Republican setback will probably give a harder edge to the vice-presidential debate. If Dick Cheney had been counting on repeating his folksy chat with Joe Lieberman in 2000, he will have to switch to attack mode. This may not work well if the personable John Edwards keeps his cool.

The turn of events bodes well for the Democrats, but the war is far from won. The Republican strategy from day one has been a relentless effort to discredit Kerry personally, and this will continue with greater fury. No distortion is too outlandish for this game. Kerry should be on solid ground to neutralize the attacks in the next two debates, especially if he keeps the focus on Bush's favoritism toward the rich. The economy is slipping back again and people are sensing the softness in the job market.

Kerry can bolster his case if he directs some of the public's attention away from the personal contest to the relative performance of the two parties. The Democrats have repeatedly inherited economic weakness from the Republicans and presided over recoveries. Average economic growth, and gains in employment, household income, and the stock market have been higher under Democratic presidents. Kerry can use this background to predict that voters will once again call on the Democrats to get the country back on track.

Recent advertising by the Kerry campaign has been encouraging, because it has cast the issues in terms of Bush and the Republicans against Kerry and the Democrats. It is refreshing to see a presidential candidate acknowledge his role as party leader. Not only does he recognize the broader value of the party label, he also helps his party's candidates for congressional and local office.

Local candidates are often reluctant to see their campaigns as part of a larger contest, but they are more dependent on that contest than they realize. Few are truly capable of swimming against the tide unless they represent a safe district. Voter knowledge of candidates is just too sketchy. Democrats running in 2004 need some political wind at their backs, and it can only come from a successful national campaign that takes advantage of Republican weakness.

# THE FORGOTTEN MAN

*October 17, 2004*

The great debates are over. John Kerry benefited from the low expectations of many casual voters, who were surprised at how direct and aggressive he was in critiquing George Bush's performance as president. Polls showed that the public considered Kerry the winner in all three and that the race was back to a dead heat. This is not good news for Bush, because Al Gore was clearly behind at this point in 2000. Moreover, the polls are probably underestimating the turnout effects of strong Democratic motivation and a surge in new voter registrations.

This will go down as one of the bitterest campaigns in history, and Kerry will get credit for hitting back hard in the final months. It will probably carry him to victory, and may produce a few surprises in the Senate and House races. It is doubtful, however, that Democrats will regain control of the House, and a 50-50 deadlock in the Senate is probably the best they can hope for. This is a pity, because Kerry's chances of getting any of his legislative proposals enacted will be slim at best. He will have to be content to veto Republican initiatives and work on clearing up the mess in our international relations.

Democrats will celebrate on election night, but a window of greater opportunity will have been lost. The weak job market, loss of family income, exploding national debt, decline of the dollar and the stock market, rise of poverty and crime, all of these provided ample evidence of the failures of the Bush Administration. But they were also indicative of a recurring pattern in American politics: Republican control has meant shifting attention to the wealthy at the expense of the middle class and working poor. The result has consistently been a weakened economy that has been resurrected only when Democrats have returned to power.

Kerry is rightly focusing on the decline of the American standard of living under Bush, but neither he nor anyone else is putting it in a larger political perspective. The result is that voters must choose between Bush's record and Kerry's promises, as well as between the candidates' styles. They are not being asked to choose between the Democratic record and the Republican record. Democratic candidates in the congressional races will try to run ahead of the national ticket, but few will do so unless they are well-entrenched incumbents. Too many Democrats have acquiesced in the Republican ridicule of their party label and have underestimated its value.

If Democrats do not think it useful to recall the economic distress that Franklin Roosevelt, John Kennedy, and Jimmy Carter inherited, one would think they would at least be anxious to recall the story of Bill Clinton's administration. Clinton took office with unemployment at seven percent, a growing budget deficit, and distressing levels of social ills such as crime, poverty, domestic violence, and teenage pregnancy. Against unanimous Republican opposition, he engineered a modest increase in corporate and high-income tax rates, a hike in the minimum wage, and a boost in the earned-income tax credit. The budget deficit began to melt, consumer demand rebounded, business confidence and investment returned, and unemployment headed downward. As the economy surged, social dysfunction retreated steadily.

So far, John Kerry has largely repeated Al Gore's neglect of the Clinton story. Clinton was given a brief time to speak on the first night of the convention, then left town. Kerry mentioned him two or three times in passing during the debates, but did not linger on the subject. Since being sidelined by a heart operation, Clinton has gone from being marginally involved in the campaign to being virtually invisible. So the strongest rationale for replacing a Republican president and Congress with a Democratic president and Congress has gone largely ignored.

Who are the geniuses that have convinced Democratic candidates to avoid association with the most popular and capable politician since John Kennedy? Al Gore could have won the election in 2000 if he had promised a continuation of the peace and prosperity that he and Clinton had presided over. Even at the nadir of Clinton's personal problems, his job approval rating remained high. The American people are not stupid. They know how to distinguish between personal matters and the well being of the country. George Bush himself has benefited from this distinction.

Harry Truman once said that if you give voters a choice between a real Republican and a phony one, they will choose the real one every time. He could have added that if Democrats are embarrassed by their party label and their most effective leader, how can they expect voters to have confidence in them. Except for the interstate highway system, virtually every benefit that Americans enjoy from government has been delivered by the Democratic Party. Why does the story go untold?

Franklin Roosevelt touched the soul of Americans in 1932, in the depths of the Great Depression, when he called the American worker "the forgotten man." The forgotten man in 2004 is Bill Clinton.

# WHAT'S IT ALL ABOUT?

*October 23, 2004*

Even the most avid political junkie will be happy to see this election fade into history. Rarely has the acrimony reached such a fever pitch, with even the spouses getting into the fray. One can imagine a playground fight, with each combatant crying to the teacher, "He started it!" "No I didn't, he did!"

We are now in a contest to see who can frighten voters the most. Scare tactics are nothing new in American politics. Republicans defeated the Democrats in the early 1950s with outlandish claims about communist infiltration of the government. John Kennedy turned the tables in 1960 by invoking a supposed missile gap in our arms race with the Soviet Union. Lyndon Johnson convinced many voters that the election of Barry Goldwater could precipitate a nuclear war. The elder George Bush used racist television ads to raise the specter of violent criminals preying on women if Michael Dukakis were elected.

This year, along with familiar Democratic warnings about the fate of Social Security, the dire consequences revolve around the threat of terrorism. George Bush and Dick Cheney talk of little else, charging that John Kerry does not understand the terrorist threat and would not take a hard line against them His election would embolden Al Qaeda and make a major attack in this country more likely. This comes from an administration that virtually ignored the warnings of on attack before September 11, 2001.

Kerry, for his part, has decried the gaps in our home-land security. He cites the millions of containers passing through our ports without inspection, lax border inspections, weak security at chemical and nuclear plants, and shortages of firemen. These shortcomings sound impressive, until we recall that not a single incident of attempted terrorism has been connected to any of them. One presumed terrorist was apprehended in 1999 as he attempted to cross the Canadian border into Washington. He aroused the suspicions of a cus-toms agent who was using the common sense procedures of the pre-9/11 era.

Opening containers in our ports would create incredible congestion and disrupt an intermodal transportation system that companies have worked for years to streamline. The resulting costs would be passed to American consumers, while the inspection process itself would resemble searching for a needle in a haystack. As for border crossings, American citizens are already treated like potential criminals, subjected to vehicle searches without probable cause. This is even more true with airline travel, which has become an ordeal to be survived. No one is spared the indignities and endless lines, not elderly couples, children, pregnant women, school girls, celebrities, no one.

Two words that are not in the lexicon of politicians or journalists are "reasonable" and "probability." The probabili-ty of a successful terrorist attack on any of the targets that are conjured up is miniscule. The probability of preventing an attack with security guards and procedures is nil. Determined terrorists, willing to commit suicide, will find a way to cause mayhem. The only way to stop them is to iden-tify them with intelligence, infiltration, and common sense awareness. Overloading Americans with security procedures is unnecessary, ineffective, unreasonable, and destructive. It has contributed to the bankruptcy of the airline industry, weakened the economy, and generally made American life less pleasant. It has been the greatest victory that Osama bin Laden could have hoped for.

Let us pray that this sterile debate will not outlive the election, and that new nonsense will not be visited upon us. In this drone of dire consequences, it is easy to lose sight of what this election is really about. This election is about taxes, debt, legitimate government services, international cooperation, and personal rights. It is about whether Americans of all backgrounds and economic status are valued or only those who have acquired or inherited wealth. It is about whether we as a community will try to solve problems or brush them off with ideology.

The primary objective of the conservative Republican leadership has been to relieve the tax burden on the wealthy. They have done this without regard to the consequences for the national debt or the shrinkage of benefits and services to low- and middle-income families. They have done so in the face of abundant evidence that the economy suffers when money is taken out of circulation by diverting it from government expenditures to the bank accounts of the rich. They have ignored the impact on state and local governments, who have raised sales and property taxes while cutting education and health services. Given another four years of power, this narrow leadership will move even more aggressively to undermine the balance of private and public enterprise that has sustained America since the Great Depression. Some are already pushing a national sales tax to replace the progressive income tax, a move that could easily precipitate another depression.

Conservative Republicans talk as if government were an octopus determined to strangle the innovative, acquisitive, entrepreneurial spirit that made America great. If this were so, how is it that the United States has remained the leading generator of great fortunes and technological change, the leading font (with the Japanese) of lifestyle innovation, and the incubator in which anything can be bought and sold. The truth is that government in this country has always fostered an environment in which capitalism could flourish. The great political battles have involved the mitigation of the ills of unbridled capitalism and the provision of needed infrastructure and services that capitalism would not support.

Before Democrat Woodrow Wilson took office in 1913, Republicans had taken the lead in creating this balance. The conservative surge that ousted Teddy Roosevelt and the progressives from the Republican Party was similar to the Goldwater-Gingrich purge of moderates in the 1970s and 1980s. This strident brand of Republicanism tries to rewrite history through the prism of economic dogma, using arguments that run counter to the logical understanding of even older Republican voters. The gradual disappearance of this older generation has been a factor in the deepening ideological divide that has come to characterize American politics.

Social Security is a basic benefit that is definitely in jeopardy if Republican control continues. Affluent conservatives have long tried to opt out of the system, and in the process have obscured its true nature. It was never intended to substitute for individual retirement planning. Social Security is a national insurance plan that assures a basic level of subsistence to retired or disabled workers and their families. The money paid into the system is a tax, not a retirement contribution. Allowing people to opt out or divert part of their share to individual retirement accounts would cause a shortfall that would force a serious cut in basic benefits.

The long-run stability of Social Security is even more threatened by the alarming budget deficits created by the

Bush tax cuts. Although technically a trust fund, it has long been used to finance government borrowing. The surplus that built in the trust fund during prosperous times has been loaned to the general fund to cover current expenses, in the process hiding the true size of the budget deficit. The combination of baby boom retirements and longer life expectancies are going to bring a time when the general fund must begin to pay back what has been borrowed from the trust fund.

At the end of the Clinton Administration, the projected surpluses in the general fund were sufficient to allay any concerns about the future viability of both Social Security and Medicare. This healthy situation has now been lost, and threatens to deteriorate steadily. Only the willingness of foreigners to buy our securities is keeping interest rates from soaring. With record trade deficits and the dollar falling, one wonders how long we can pull this rabbit out of the hat. It is sobering to realize that the largest purchaser of U.S. government bonds is now China.

It is tempting to speculate that the reckless fiscal irresponsibility of the Bush Republicans is a deliberate plan to bankrupt Social Security, Medicare, and the federal government in general. The more ideological among them have said as much. If so, the American people have much to lose in this election. How many average Americans really want to sacrifice their economic security, consumer protection, environmental safeguards, educational opportunity, workplace safety, national parks, confidence in air traffic control, or the other public benefits they have taken for granted?

The decline of America's reputation and the breakdown of international cooperation may be related as much to George Bush's personality as to Republican doctrine. It is one area where the business community is not comfortable with the course of events. Before the invasion of Iraq, globalism was the watchword of economic conservatives - the opportunities of the global marketplace and the desirability of freely deploying capital, labor, and technology across national boundaries. While the global economy is still intact, the decline of confidence in America's leadership and fiscal policies is unsettling. It also threatens to undermine efforts to combat terrorism. Success in this struggle depends on cooperation among the intelligence and law-enforcement services of the world. In a larger sense, it depends on the attractiveness of the free and democratic culture that we and our friends represent as an alternative to extremism. Victory in the cold war with communism was a cultural victory, and victory in this war will be the same.

Americans who value individual freedom have a large stake in this election. The next president will probably nominate two or three justices to the Supreme Court, a court that is already cool to personal liberty. Republican philosophy has always combined economic freedom with social conformity. The Bush Republicans, anxious to hold their conservative religious supporters, will opt for nominees who take this preference to extremes. A woman's right to choose an abortion will clearly be threatened. The rights of defendants will be curtailed, unless they are corporate defendants, in which case the rights of plaintiffs may be curtailed. Gay rights and discrimination law will likely be weakened. Little is being said about this, perhaps because the political calculation is complex. The future of the federal judiciary is, however, one of the key issues in this campaign.

# WHY KERRY WILL WIN

*October 31, 2004*

Today is Halloween, so I might as well do something scary. I'll go out on a limb and make a prediction. John Kerry will win the presidency, and by enough of a margin that no long dispute will be needed. This is not just wishful thinking. It is an assessment based on all the available indicators and the perspective of history.

Let us begin with the polls. The average is showing Bush with a slight lead in the national popular vote. The most reliable, however, the Zogby tracking poll, is showing a tie. This is better than Al Gore showed three days before the 2000 election. The difference is probably the return of some Ralph Nader voters to the Democratic fold.

The polls, however, are probably missing part of the story. There has been a surge of new voter registrations among young people, African-Americans, and Hispanics, groups that are consistently undersampled in polling. Available data suggests that Kerry holds double digit leads among all the groups of new voters. Of course, registration does not guarantee voting, so everyone is coming to agree that turnout will be the decisive factor in this close election.

It comes down to motivation. A week of early voting in Georgia demonstrated this. With a handful of voting locations open, lines formed to create 2- to 3-hour waits. Many voters took a look and decided to wait until Election Day.

Remarkably, well over 200,000 people persevered to cast their ballots. The heaviest participation occurred in Dekalb County, which is majority African-American and solidly Democratic. The mobilization effort among black voters appeared to be well organized through churches and community organizations. It gave the appearance of a collective determination to make a difference.

Election Day is promising more of the same. With an estimated 25 percent increase nationally in the number of people planning to vote, the availability of polling places, machines, and poll workers appears seriously inadequate. Two-hour waits can be expected in many places, worse if voter challenges are widespread or technological problems crop up with new voting systems. In such conditions, determination to be counted will be a critical factor in the willingness of voters to tough it out.

What could this mean for the outcome? Conventional wisdom has always been that unfavorable voting conditions favored the Republicans, because their overall higher affluence made it easier for them to vote and also made them more conscious of the importance of voting. The Democratic electorate, more dependent on wage earners and people with transportation problems, is assumed to be less dependable and more easily discouraged. The conventional wisdom may prevail this year, but there are reasons to believe it will not.

In the fifty years that I have been following elections, I have never seen such intensity of feeling against a Republican candidate. George W. Bush has done what John Kerry could not do, what even Bill Clinton could not do, aroused an unwavering determination among Democrats to defeat a Republican president. This determination reaches beyond identifiable Democrats into the ranks of younger people who have participated marginally or not at all in the process up to now.

What are the sources of this groundswell? Part of it is lingering resentment over the 2000 election. Democrats believe that the will of the people was frustrated by an archaic electoral system and manipulation by the Florida administration of Jeb Bush and a Republican majority on the Supreme Court. African-American voters, in particular, believe that many of them were denied the opportunity to vote or their votes discounted by partisan administrations. They are using this as a rallying cry to arouse their communities in 2004.

The closeness of the 2000 election was also a wake-up call to young people who thought their vote did not really matter, one out of millions. But for them, Iraq seems to be the overriding issue. Many see the invasion as a moral issue, an attempt to force our will on people who do not share our cultural roots. Young people are incensed not just by the loss of life and limb among their peers, but also by the devastation wrought on the Iraqi people. The dissimulation by the Bush Administration about the motives for war has confirmed their distrust of the establishment, and fueled speculation that a return to the draft may be in the works after the election.

Is all of this enough to bring them to the voting booth? Without question, only a portion of the newly registered will follow through. My sense is that the portion will be large enough to affect the outcome in close states.

The state of the economy is the remaining factor producing anti-Bush intensity. Unemployment is up, but even more significant is the number of people who were doing well when Bush took office and have spent two or three years trying to scrape by with free lance, temporary, or lower-paying jobs. The consequence of public policy for the health of the economy has been demonstrated in a way that was not made apparent in 2000. The number of people who will persevere to cast a protest vote against poor economic performance may not be extremely large, but it does not have to be to tip a close election.

Will this level of motivation be offset by an equal determination to defend the president? Loyal Republican voters, those who do not miss elections, will not miss this one. Nor will the politicized members of conservative churches, especially with gay marriage amendments on many state ballots. For Republican candidates, the cause for worry is the pool of less committed, less attentive voters who lean to Bush because of his tough talk about terrorism and his general good-old-boy manner.

Many of these people have seen their economic situation stagnate or deteriorate in the past few years. They have seen plant closings in small cities and have friends who have lost jobs and health insurance. They still support Bush, but without much enthusiasm. This shows up in polls that give Bush a job approval rating of less than 50 percent. Polls have also shown that Kerry supporters attribute much greater importance to this election than Bush supporters do.

If the NASCAR fans, NFL couch potatoes, sports bar patrons, and harried soccer moms decide not to bother with long lines at the polling places, Republican turnout may be less than expected. The party mobilization effort has relied heavily on telephone and mail reminders, and this may not overcome the disincentive of crowded polling places. It is hardly a substitute for the strong anti-Bush sentiment that is fueling the Kerry vote.

So I am going to stick my neck out and predict that Kerry will not only win the popular vote, but will carry most of the key battleground states as well. The trend may be apparent earlier than expected, although delayed polling place closings could make for slow reporting of returns. If turnout is especially high in Democratic precincts, those returns may be late in reporting, giving a misleading impression in the early results. It could be a long and interesting night.

# POST MORTEM

*November 4, 2004*

I was wrong. I bought into the theory that the Democrats
and their assorted allies could out-mobilize the Republicans.
I assumed that anti-Bush intensity would trump pro-Bush
intensity. I thought that despite the flaws of their candidate
and their inability to get the dialogue away from terrorism,
the Democrats were at least going to make it in the presidential race. I thought that young people were finally going
to make a difference.

Democrats have Ralph Nader to thank for putting
George W. Bush in the White House. They have an obscure
judge in Massachusetts to thank for keeping him there. In
the hour of his darkest need, she came to his rescue. When
the debate over a national constitutional amendment banning gay marriage seemed to subside late in the summer, it
was easy to miss what was going on below the surface.

The circus following the Massachusetts decision put
state constitutional amendments on the ballot in eleven
states, including critical Ohio. If the war in Iraq had given
Democrats the spark to boost the turnout of young people,
gay marriage was a tinderbox for the Republicans. Evangelical
Christians responded to the appeals pressed through their
church networks. They turned out in record numbers and
voted heavily for Republicans. It was enough to offset a
strong, although slightly disappointing, turnout of 18-29 year
olds, and it tipped Ohio to Bush. That was the ballgame.

It was clear from exit polling that many voters were motivated not by economic issues or Iraq, but by something loosely characterized as "moral values." There does appear to be a simmering cultural divide in the country between people who value conformity and aggressive patriotism and those who are more open to personal differences and international understanding. Both have roots in the American experience.

The frontier image of the close-knit, self-reliant family remains the model for many Americans, especially in small towns. They cling to it even when it is belied by their own situations, just as they keep faith in their religion despite trials. On the other hand, America's urban history of immigration from a variety of cultures, while often a source of tension, has produced a culture of tolerance. Open-mindedness has become its own badge of honor for American intellectuals, who do not always hide their contempt for the bible-readers and NASCAR fans.

Republicans have long used this cultural divide to their advantage, and are constantly on the lookout for issues to crystallize it. Party professionals do not really want a cultural war, and many do not even share the emotions of their followers. What they want is to see the resentment expressed in the voting booth, after which people can return to civility. Safely in power, the Republican establishment can pursue its economic goals while dropping a few crumbs to religious conservatives.

For a Democrat, it is frustrating to know that most of these voters would be better served if they resisted the cynical manipulation of their feelings by the likes of Karl Rove. Nothing in George W. Bush's family background or the first 40 years of his life suggests that he has anything in common with the voters who put him over the top. His protestations of faith in God sound as clever and calculated as his locker room talk about foreign policy. Faced with failure in a war, however, he may have convinced himself that his policies are divinely inspired. If so, I pray for my country.

Democrats have had difficulty with the cultural issues. Many of their active constituents feel as strongly about tolerance and personal liberty as conservatives feel about conformity. John Kerry tried to satisfy both sides but sounded unconvincing. Nor did it seem that the cultural issues could be overcome simply by focusing on job losses. In the end, Democrats face the same dilemma with these issues as they do with tax issues. The Republicans have simple, coherent positions, and Democrats have tried to get close to those positions without embracing them. In so doing, they cloud the rationale for Democratic opposition. As George Bush said, "I don't do nuances."

The fundamentalist foray into politics is grounded in the teachings of the Old Testament. When one looks at the ministry of Jesus, a quite different message of public morality emerges. It is one of compassion, tolerance, forgiveness, and concern for the welfare of others. It is one of inclusion rather than exclusion. Democrats can discuss religious principles as comfortably as Republicans can if they focus on the heart of Christianity. In that context, their policies hold up pretty well.

Many in the Democratic Party are hoping for a savior, a Democratic version of Ronald Reagan. For a while, it seemed that Bill Clinton would be the savior, but Clinton's popularity never translated into gains for the party. Then his personal scandal frightened Democratic candidates, who failed to capitalize on the contrast between Clinton prosperity and Bush decline. They did not use their best argument.

This is no time to begin the process of speculating on the next presidential candidate. I am not going to pretend that the solution for the Democratic Party is simple or foolproof, but I think it is clear that the party has not established a coherent image in the minds of recent generations of voters comparable to what it had with older generations. Democrats have a history of achievement with a philosophy behind it. They cannot, however, expect generations of voters to absorb it through osmosis.

Current issues do not exist in a vacuum, most of them also have a history. Why do we have Social Security, and why is it important to preserve its structure? Why do we have Medicare? Why did we adopt environmental laws and fuel economy standards? Why do we have fair labor standards with overtime pay? Why did the Supreme Court uphold a woman's right to have an abortion? Why do we have affirmative action and what is it really supposed to mean? Why do we have a progressive income tax instead of a national sales tax? Why are Democrats for these things and Republicans against them?

We never hear Democratic candidates answer these questions. The Democratic National Committee does not spend any of its millions of dollars telling these stories. The Senate and House Campaign Committees do not tell them. The Democratic campaign in 2004 was almost entirely an attack on George Bush and his failures. Even if it had succeeded in turning him out, it would not have reversed the fortunes of the Democratic Party. Something else is needed to do that.

Many Democratic candidates, including the senate minority leader, tried to overcome the deficit of their national ticket by taking Republican positions on several issues. Except for a few well-entrenched incumbents, it was an exercise in futility. The party needs good candidates, of course, and certainly not ones who are liabilities. The fate of these candidates, however, will be determined more by the success of the party than their own personal campaigns. As a collection of individuals running for office, the Democratic Party will not emerge from its current situation.

Even at the presidential level, where it is impossible to escape the focus on personal attributes, cultivating a meaningful image of the Democratic Party would help any candidate. In several columns, I warned of the danger of letting the 2004 election become a personality contest. If this campaign demonstrated anything, it was that even personal strengths can be turned against a candidate. Republican strategists are masters at picking up on contradictions or awkward phrases, then using them to disparage a candidate. A person's record can be easily distorted, and correcting the distortions is usually a fruitless effort.

Presidential candidates who insist on running only as individuals run a great risk. John Kerry was never able to generate warmth among the American people, and he was never able to explain his votes on the Iraq war resolution and the supplemental appropriation for the war. He came close to winning only because of hostility toward George Bush. Personal skeletons might have prevented Bill Clinton from becoming president if not for the candidacy of Ross Perot. Energizing the party label and making the election more of a party contest can help overcome a candidate's vulnerabilities.

The Democratic Party is faced once again with a need for soul-searching. Past efforts have not produced consensus, and it will be difficult to do so this time. When an athlete is going through a slump, he or she eventually goes back to basics. It is time for the Democratic Party to do the same. Why did it take the positions it did in the past and are they still relevant? If they are, how can we communicate their relevance? If people are going to identify themselves as Democrats, they need reasons - reasons that make sense in their lives. They need to know that voting for a Democrat is logical even if they do not know the candidate or have some reservations about him or her.

Democrats in the House and Senate will, hopefully, dig in to resist the dismantling of their legacy. In the process, they should spend some of their money and use their best spokespeople to argue their case before the American people. They should make sure that people hear what is at stake. This is the best way to give voters an alternative to the cultural debate fostered by the Republicans.

*Addendum*

# WHY TAX CUTS FAIL

George W. Bush began his reign over a Republican Congress predictably in 2003 by proposing another round of tax cuts. Its centerpiece, the elimination of taxes on corporate dividends, is patently regressive. Like another Republican favorite, the elimination of estate taxes, it would deliver most of its benefits to high-income taxpayers. By most estimates, about half the lost revenue would go to the top one percent of households. As with the 2001 cuts, Bush and his allies in Congress claimed their program would stimulate economic growth by encouraging investment. As 2004 drew to a close, however, neither the stock market, consumer confidence, nor the level of employment had returned to where they were when Bush took office in January 2001. It is thus appropriate to ask whether such tax cuts, or for that matter any tax cuts, are likely to help the economy out of its sluggish performance.

Bush's 2001 tax cut program, passed with scattered Democratic support, included rebates of up to $600 of prior year taxes. Many economists considered these rebates to be a reasonable way to stimulate the economy. Although they gave little or nothing to low-income families, their benefits were spread relatively evenly across the rest of the population. It was assumed that middle-income taxpayers would spend their rebates and rekindle demand for cell phones, computers, running shoes, and all the other things that create jobs for somebody. When the dust had settled, however, it appeared that even these well-intentioned tax rebates had done little to help the economy.

Overall, according to a careful study done at the University of Michigan, only about 25 percent of recipients spent most of the money. The rest put it in savings accounts or paid off debt, and told researchers that they had no intention of spending it in the year ahead. Why the reluctance to spend a check received from the U.S. Treasury? It seems that expectations play an important role. People tend to view tax rebates and refunds as windfalls rather than genuine increases in their income. If they feel secure and optimistic, and are not burdened by debt, they will spend most of the money. If they are paying high interest charges or are worried about the future, they will pay down debt or save the money. They will also save or invest the money if they have no particular need for it, which is true for many high-income taxpayers.

Interestingly, one reason that tax cuts are viewed as windfalls is that many people, from all income brackets, are skeptical about future tax policy. They suspect that what is given today may be taken back tomorrow, as government budgets go deeper into red ink. They are skeptical with good reason, because that is what happened in 1990 and 1993, albeit with much political agony. Moreover, the Bush rebates and rate cuts for the middle class have already been partly soaked up by increased sales and property taxes at the state and local level. The American public may be much maligned for its disinterest in politics, but it has consistently demonstrated more maturity on the subject of taxation than politicians have. People believe that you do not get something for nothing, and they know that they depend on government for many important things. Sooner or later, those have to be paid for, the voodoo economists notwithstanding.

One could argue that reducing debt or increasing savings will make the economy healthier in the future, and there is some truth to that. It does not help in the short run, however, and in fact may hurt by reducing liquidity, that is, the circulation of money. This brings us back to basics.

## Economics 101

Economic activity occurs when goods or property or services are exchanged among people. Economic growth occurs when the total value of such exchanges increases, either because of an increase in population or because of an acceleration in the pace of transactions. Because we have largely abandoned the barter form of transaction, the pace of economic activity is best represented by the velocity of circulation of money.

From a purely economic standpoint, it matters little what the money is spent on. It could be houses, cars, comic books, movie tickets, restoration of wetlands, road construction, manicures, or salaries for teachers. From a community standpoint, governments must take responsibility for some transactions that would not otherwise occur. Whether decisions are made collectively or individually, however, prosperity (defined as full employment and rising real incomes) depends on the rapidity with which goods, services, and property are exchanged for money.

The great English economist John Maynard Keynes has often been praised and often condemned, but because of his impenetrable style, rarely read. During the depths of the Great Depression, he wrestled with the phenomenon of involuntary unemployment and concluded, among other things, that employment depended on a society's propensity to consume. That propensity was in turn determined by both objective and subjective (psychological) factors. Simplifying and updating Keynes' insight, the decisions of individuals to spend money are a function of their ability to spend, their need to spend, and their willingness to spend.

A low-income family does not consider buying a house because they do not have the means to do so. They will, however, spend virtually all their income with little delay, because their basic needs absorb it quickly. They do not waste much time pondering discretionary expenditures. As we move up the income chain, options increase and psychological factors become more important in decisions to save or spend.

For middle-income families, much of their income is committed to purposes that have taken on the character of basic needs: mortgage payments, car payments, life insurance, dental care, air conditioning, etc. Other purchases stem from a reluctance to say no to their children. Until the children are out of college, the savings of these families are created primarily by education planning and automatic contributions to retirement plans. For families in such situations, the security of knowing they can meet these obligations is a critical component of their spending decisions. Dependability of income is a foremost concern. If the family is apprehensive about this, tax rebates or refunds are likely to be saved or used to reduce debt. Only if the family is optimistic about its financial condition and prospects will such windfalls be used for discretionary spending.

Higher-income families have less concern, if any, about security, so they are theoretically free to spend tax cuts at will. The question is whether they have any immediate need to spend. The higher up the ladder they are perched, the less likely they are to have unfulfilled desires waiting to be satisfied. Moreover, their spending habits may well include luxury automobiles, foreign residences, and travel, consumption that sends much of the money abroad.

The principal deterrent to consumption by high-income families, however, is their preoccupation with investment. At some point on the income ladder, the accumulation of wealth becomes an end in itself and maximizing returns from investment becomes an absorbing challenge. Perhaps recognizing this, the so-called supply-side economists have tried to justify tax cuts for the rich by arguing that they increase the level of investment and thus create jobs. The fallacy of this argument is that returns on investment are best when the economy is growing and capital is in demand. If the economy is stagnant or shrinking, corporations have excess capacity and little need for capital. Cash accumulates in the accounts of both corporations and wealthy individuals, waiting for consumer demand to pick up. Thus, in a weak economy, tax cut for the rich takes money out of circulation.

This effect can be seen in the balance sheets of major corporations. Since the first Bush tax cuts took effect, Microsoft has doubled its cash and short-term interest-bearing investments to $60 billion. General Motors has more than doubled its own to $50 billion. General Electric, as of September 2004, had accumulated $135 billion, compared to just $9 billion in December 2001. All of these companies have paid lower taxes as a percentage of revenue during the Bush Administration. Because of weak demand, however, they have accumulated capital rather than investing it in job-creating activity. Microsoft finally paid out half its cash as a special dividend, a handsome reward to its executives holding large numbers of shares.

The conclusion of all this is that tax cuts, if they stimulate economic growth at all, will do so only when the economy is already healthy. In a weak economy, they will just take money out of circulation and further reduce the pace of economic activity. The resources would be much more effective if placed into the economy through government spending. This is especially true because governments incur deficits during economic slowdowns that force them to spend revenue virtually as soon as it comes in. A very large proportion of government expenditures finds its way quickly into wages and salaries, helping the recovery of consumption.

## Economic Balance

Over a period of time, a market economy will seek balance, and it has proved to be the most efficient model for allocating labor and resources to productive uses. A concern with free market economies, however, is their tendency to alternate between expansion and contraction. Strong investment returns repeatedly generate overcapacity, which depresses prices and forces companies to reduce employment.

As Keynes pointed out, consumption patterns help to mitigate these swings and bring them back toward balance. When real incomes are rising, consumption lags behind, moderating the expansion. When real incomes fall, savings and debt are used to maintain consumption, moderating the decline. Government spending follows a similar pattern, accumulating surpluses in good times and incurring deficits in recessions. Keynes considered this a beneficial pattern, which should be appreciated by politicians. Unfortunately, few politicians are perceptive or courageous enough to follow his precepts. They are prone to rebate surpluses instead of saving them for the inevitable downturn. Moreover, state constitutions generally require balanced budgets, and are thus inherently anti-Keynesian during recessions.

Nonetheless, the model had a chance to work in the 1990s. Modest tax increases on high incomes, recycled into the economy by increased government spending and an increase in the Earned Income Tax Credit, promoted a recovery. The thriving economy of the Clinton years boosted tax revenues and reduced the contribution that government debt had been making to the money supply. As deficits turned to surpluses at the end of the decade, the economy began to cool and might have smoothed out with a soft landing if the Federal Reserve had not administered shock treatment by driving short-term interest rates up sharply.

It follows that the Bush approach to stimulating economic growth is precisely the wrong one. Instead of cutting government revenue, federal spending should be increased to create jobs. Since 2001, state and local governments have been struggling desperately to balance budgets decimated by the recession. At the very time that job creation was needed, teaching positions were being eliminated in alarming numbers, along with an array of other public service jobs. These losses would have had a greater impact if they had not been offset somewhat by increased federal spending on the military and homeland security. Ironically, most of the modest employment gain during 2004 was in the government sector.

An increase in federal borrowing is an acceptable way to boost spending in the short run, but a more effective strategy is to increase tax rates on high incomes. This is not the burden that some would have us believe. One of the ironies of the 1990s was that the Clinton tax increase of 1993 and the resulting modest redistribution of income fueled a pace of economic growth that increased the wealth of the wealthy. Low- and middle-income families benefited from the robust job market, but high-income families actually increased their share of national income.

## A Question of Confidence

The use of tax cuts to stimulate economic growth or recovery runs aground because it does not alter a basic reality: the pace of economic activity depends heavily on confidence. Low-income families will spend available income, but the level of spending by the broad middle class will reflect its confidence in future economic conditions. The same holds for businesses. No tax incentives will entice business-men to increase capital spending or hire workers if they do not anticipate growing demand for their products or servic-es.

Confidence is influenced strongly by the perceptions people acquire in their places of work or business. It does not take long for them to sense a deterioration in the labor market and begin to act accordingly. It does not take a very large swing in consumer and investor confidence to turn economic growth into stagnation. Confidence also seems to have a political dimension. Although not many Americans remain who associate the Republican Party with the onset of the Great Depression, a significant number do recognize that they have been better off under Democratic presidents than Republicans. Public opinion polls consistently show more confidence in Democratic economic leadership.

This public perception is based firmly on historical experience. Since World War II, eight of the country's ten recessions have occurred under Republican presidents. Since 1948, the average unemployment rate has been more than a percentage point higher under Republican presidents, while the annual rate of job growth has been substantially lower. Nor has this been offset by lower inflation, since consumer prices have risen faster under Republican administrations than under Democratic ones.

A prolonged slump in the stock market began after Labor Day in 2000, when polls began to forecast a Republican victory in the presidential election. Despite Wall Street's faith that Bush's election would boost the market, it never happened. The president and a Republican Congress proceeded on a crusade to lower taxes, turning budget pro-jections from black to red. Supply-siders filled the airways with predictions of an economic miracle that would wipe out the deficits, but too many people remembered this hoax from the 1980s. Investors and corporate executives gave the required lip service to conservative principles, but sat on their money rather than risking it.

## The Lessons of the Reagan Administration

Republicans habitually speak about the Reagan Administration as a golden age, hoping perhaps that younger Americans will accept the idea without question. Their parents, however, may be forgiven for not remembering it that way. Average economic growth in the 1980s was the lowest of any decade since the Great Depression, and consumer spending the lowest since World War II. The illusion of prosperity was created in the mid-1980s by heavy military spending that benefited certain industries and certain parts of the country. In the meantime, traditional industries of the Midwestern rustbelt suffered, and the collapse of oil prices spread financial distress through Texas, Colorado, Utah, and Appalachia. Speculation in real estate and complicated financial instruments led to scandals and massive bank failures.

The 1980s are an instructive period for understanding how misguided government policy can disrupt balance in the economy. Tax cuts tailored for the rich and corporations shifted real income to those least likely to spend it, aggravating the gulf between rich and poor. As deficits mounted in the 80s, the lost tax revenue was borrowed back at high interest rates, further enriching wealthy purchasers of government bonds. The dollar fell precipitously, making imports expensive and allowing the high-flying Japanese to buy American property and companies. High real interest rates eventually depressed consumer spending and corporate investment, leading to a spectacular collapse of stock prices in October 1987. Ultimately, areas like California and Massachusetts, which had prospered from the defense buildup, sank into recessions as the national credit card was overdrawn. Reagan's successor, the elder George Bush, lost his reelection bid under the cloud of widespread unemployment.

The Reagan and Bush administrations practiced reckless fiscal policies that were counterintuitive for most Americans. They drove the national debt from an acceptable one trillion dollars to an unacceptable four trillion. Bill Clinton was forced to use much of his political capital to bring the budget under control and real interest rates down. The result was that the country prospered again because balance and confidence were restored.

Supply-side economics proved to be a hoax, but demand-side economics is definitely not a hoax. Increased purchasing power at the lower rungs of the economic ladder ripples up through the economy. When a poor person is able to buy an eight year-old car, the seller can step up to a four year-old car, and the sellers of those can buy new cars. If the poor person can afford to maintain his car, the market for auto parts will improve. Such examples are plentiful throughout the economy.

For a market economy to function efficiently and provide sustained growth over the long term, it needs stability in government policy. The American people have come to expect an array of services from government and the majority is realistic about the need to pay for those services. The economy can perform perfectly well with a substantial public sector, as long as that sector is predictable and adequately financed. The accumulation of surpluses during good times works against speculative investment and the inevitable deficits during slowdowns help to support personal income.

As George W. Bush begins his second term, the economy is struggling to find some cyclical traction. The official unemployment rate has fallen a little, but many people have dropped out of the labor force after fruitless job searches. The persistence of a weak job market is eroding the social gains of the 1990s, as crime rates and family instability have begun rising again. America has become alarmingly dependent on foreign creditors, a situation that could provoke a crisis if the dollar continues to fall. If the Republican majority persists with an illogical fiscal policy, as seems likely, there is considerable risk that the economy will drift and could slip backward.

## References

Matthew D. Shapiro and Joel Slemrod, *Consumer Response to Tax Rebates.* University of Michigan Department of Economics, October 2002.

John Maynard Keynes, *The General Theory of Employment, Interest, and Money.* Amherst, NY, Prometheus Books, 1997.

*About the Author*

Kenneth R. Libbey has a Ph.D. in political science from Syracuse University and taught at the University of Cincinnati. For 20 years, he evaluated government programs as a member of the U.S. General Accounting Office. In 1998, he ran for the state senate in Oregon. He is the author of *I Forgot, Honey, Why Are We Democrats?* He now lives and writes in Decatur, Georgia.